A Beginner's Journey to Ethereum's Smart Contracts

[Engineering Smart Contracts and DApps in Solidity and Web3.Js]

By

[Peter Namisiko Wanjala]

First Edition: [April 2018]
Printed in the United States of America
ISBN: [9781980877288]

Executive Summary

The potentials of Ethereum smart contracts—powered by the ubiquitous Blockchain technology—has been the subject of raging debate in recent times. Pundits have long held the argument that smart contracts hold the promise of curing hurdles associated with financial contracts, banking transactions, e-commerce, logistics, supply chain and legal contracts.

It is no secret that reliance on classical contracts—which uses physical documents—has led to delays in transactions, inefficiencies, and exposures to fraudulent activities. Employing smart contracts can help companies lower administration costs, reduce risks, and promote efficient business operations across multiple sectors of the economy.

However, to appreciate these benefits and develop better smart contracts, developers have understood how to use the technologies to engineer Blockchain projects. This book provides a big picture view of engineering Ethereum smart contracts.

It delves deeper to explore how Solidity and Web3.Js can be used to build enterprise-level smart contracts and DApps. The book has been structured into 11 chapters as follows:

- *Chapter 1: Overview of Blockchain and smart contracts*. It explores the basic concepts about Blockchain, cryptography, smart contracts, and DApps to provide you with a solid understanding on what is required to start creating smart contracts.

- **Chapter 2: Introduction to Solidity**. It delves into basic programming in Solidity.
- **Chapter 3: Smart Contracts with Web3.Js**. It introduces you to Web3.Js and how you can use it to start building smart contracts.
- **Chapter 4: Smart Contracts Events with Web3.Js**. You will learn all the basics of applying smart contract events in Web3.Js.
- **Chapter 5: Functions, mappings, and structs**. It explores the Solidity's functions, mappings and structs and how to use them to enhance the development of smart contracts.
- **Chapter 6: Inheritance and Deployment**. It examines how smart contracts can be inherited and deployed on the Ethereum Virtual Machine (EVM).
- **Chapter 7: Embark Framework**. It examines the Embark framework and how it can fast-track the development and deployment of smart contracts on EVM.
- **Chapter 8: Testing Smart Contracts**. It explores how smart contracts can be tested in different environments.
- **Chapter 9: Contracts Management with Factories**. It examines how factories can be used to manage multiple smart contracts.
- **Chapter 10: IPFS and Web Hosting**. It introduces the Interplanetary File System protocol and how it can be leveraged to host smart contracts.
- **Chapter 11: End-to-end Development of DApps**. It summarizes the various steps involved in the development of DApps.

iv

Ultimately, the focus of this book is an exploration of all aspects of smart contracts and DApps that you need to know for you to start creating Ethereum-based Blockchain projects. Let's get started.

About This Book and Assumptions

This book delves deeper into the latest technologies required to provide you with a big picture view of how to start coding Ethereum smart contracts and DApps. You will find it difficult to believe that I have assumed everything about you—after all, I have never met you!

Although most assumptions that I have about you are just silly, I believe they are the starting point if you want to get started with coding of Ethereum smart contracts and DApps. This book is about engineering smart contracts and DApps in Solidity and Web3.Js. Therefore, even though no prior experience with Solidity and Web3.Js are required, elementary knowledge and experience in the following areas are required:

- Cryptography;
- Financial management; and
- Linux commands and basic administration skills.

Besides, you will be required to have mastered at least the following programming languages:

- Java;
- JavaScript; and
- Python.

To provide you with maximum information about engineering smart contracts and DApps, the book won't dwell on platform-specific issues. Therefore, you must know how to use your favorite OS platform to install various software that we will use in the book.

TABLE OF CONTENTS

Executive Summary iii
About This Book and Assumptions............................ vi
This page has been left blank intentionally......................xii
Chapter 1: Overview of Blockchain and Ethereum
Smart Contracts 1
  Prerequisites 1
  Theory... 1
    What is Blockchain? 2
    So, what is Blockchain? 5
    How Blockchain works 6
    Cryptography and Blockchain 7
    Types of Blockchains 13
    Popular Blockchains...14
    Ethereum and smart contracts 16
    Example of a smart contract.................................17
    Differences between smart contracts and DApps
   21
    What are the various use cases for smart
    contracts? 26
  Summary..29
Chapter 2: Introduction to Solidity 30
  Lab Task 30
  Overview of Remix 31
    Types of variables in Solidity.................................35
    Smart contract constructors 36
  Lab challenge 38
  Summary..38
  References 39
Chapter 3: Smart Contracts with Web3.Js..................41
  Prerequisites 41
  Theory..41
    Basic terminologies used in DApps programming
   41

Development platforms 44
Overview of Web3.Js 46
Aim 49
Lab Activity 49
Installing Web3.Js.. 57
Remix IDE configuration 59
Start Ganache 60
Launching Web3.Js 62
Lab challenge 66
Summary.. 69
References 69
Chapter 4: Smart Contract Events with Web3.Js 71
Prerequisites 71
Theory... 71
Aim 78
Lab Activity 79
Exploring the current smart contract 79
Defining the Smart Contract Event 85
Updating the UI.. 87
Lab challenge 90
Summary.. 90
References 91
Chapter 5: Functions, Mappings, and Structs 92
Prerequisites 92
Theory... 92
#1: Functions 92
#2: Mappings 93
#3: Structs 95
Aim 99
Lab Task 1 100
#1: Smart contract 100
#2: Smart contract modifier 101
#3: Using the modifier 103
Lab Task 2 104

#1: Create a Structs 104

#2: Create a mapping 105

#3: Map additions 106

Lab challenge 107

Summary 108

References 108

Chapter 6: Inheritance and Deployment 110

Prerequisites 110

Theory 110

#1: Inheritance 110

#2: Deployment 115

Aim 117

#1: Current smart contract 117

#2: How to inherit in Solidity 119

#3: Deploying smart contracts 124

Lab challenge 131

Summary 132

References 133

Chapter 7: Embark Framework and Its Deployment

.... 134

Prerequisite 134

Theory 134

#1: EVM Blockchain 135

#2: IPFS 136

#3: Decentralized Communication (Whisper,
Orbit) 136

#4: Web Technologies 137

Using smart contracts in Embark framework 137

#1: Using Contracts 137

#2: EmbarkJS 140

#3: Embark communication 142

#4: Testing 142

Aim 143

Lab Task 144

#1: Installing Embark 144
#2: How to use Embark... 146
#3: How to deploy smart contracts..................... 152
Lab Challenge 156
Summary.. 156
References 157
Chapter 8: Solidity and Smart Contracts' Testing 158
Prerequisites 158
Theory.. 158
Overview of software testing.............................. 158
Aim 165
#1: Install Mocha 166
#2: Create the smart contract............................ 166
#3: Testing the smart contract 168
Lab challenge 171
Summary.. 171
References 172
Chapter 9: Contracts Management with Factories 173
Prerequisites 173
Theory.. 173
#1: Dynamic contract factories......................... 174
#2: Counterfactual contract deployment........ 176
#3: Arbitrary code execution on the deployed
contracts.. 177
Aim 178
Lab Task 178
#1: Create a smart contract 179
#2: Create factories.. 179
Lab challenge 182
Summary.. 183
References 184
Chapter 10: IPFS Online Files Hosting 185
Prerequisites 185
Theory.. 185

Content addressing 186

HTTP verses. IPFS 187

IPFS Objects 188

Aim 190

Lab Task 190

   #1: Install IPFS 190

   #2: How to use IPFS 191

Summary.. 192

References 192

Chapter 11: End-To-End Development of DApps ... 194

Prerequisites 194

Theory.. 194

   The architecture of DApps.................................. 196

   #1: Choose the technology 198

Aim 199

   #1: Choose the technology 200

   #2: Lab task (Set up the project) 201

   #3: Code the DApp 203

   #4: Deploy and test the DApp 203

   #5: Launch the DApp 204

Lab challenge 205

Summary.. 205

References 205

This page has been left blank intentionally

Chapter 1: Overview of Blockchain and Ethereum Smart Contracts

Prerequisites

This chapter will include programming assignments in the Solidity language. No prior experience with Solidity is required. However, elementary programming course or prior experience with programming such as Java, JavaScript or Python may be required. Besides elementary programming, other requirements include:

- Cryptography; and
- Financial management

Theory

Computer systems that run on Blockchains are disrupting several industries such as financial, health and supply chain. However, a lot of the hype around what are often called smart contracts has largely remained just that: a brand-new minefield. As such, developers, technologists and scientists are just starting to figure out how to code them to drive the next wave of revolution after the Internet.

Even though smart contract programming may look simple, there are lots of nuisances that may prove disastrous if done incorrectly. This chapter delves deeper to provide you an overview of smart contract fundamentals.

What is Blockchain?

Before we dive deeper into the mechanics of Blockchain, let's rethink how modern businesses operate.

Businesses derive immense benefits from connectivity. Essentially a business must connect with their customers, suppliers, partners and even partners if it wants to promote its bottom line. In most cases, these participants are located in different geographical and regulatory boundaries.

For instance, a company such as Amazon must establish a connection to a diverse set of participants who are often in different jurisdictions. And it's not just about connection.

A system that records the transactions and contracts must be maintained if businesses want to promote their bottom line. Obviously, proper connectivity—that allows goods and services to flow across the network— generates wealth for these firms. Markets—which are central to wealth creation—can be:

- Public: a public market can be a car auction or a fruit market; and
- Private: a private market may include supply chain financing and bonds.

As it's expected, where there markets and wealth creation, asset transfer and value is crucial. The diagram below summarizes the different categories that can be transferred:

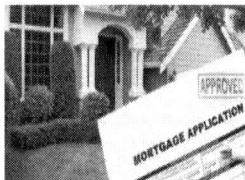

Two fundamental types of asset	Intangible assets subdivide	Cash is also an asset
• Tangible, e.g. a house • Intangible, e.g. a mortgage	• Financial, e.g. bond • Intellectual, e.g. patents • Digital, e.g. music	• Has property of anonymity

Source: IBM

By now, you are familiar with a ledger and how it's used in the financial industry. Essentially, a ledger is simply a record for a given firm. Companies will always have multiple ledgers for multiple business networks where they participate. Each ledger usually stores the following:

- Transactions: An asset transfer onto or off the ledger. For instance, Alice sells her car to Bob;
- Contracts: These are conditions that must be specified for any transaction to take place. For example, if Bob pays money for the purchase of the car to Alice, then a car passes ownership from Alice to Bob. If the car isn't functioning, then the funds may not be released to Bob.

Transactions and contracts have primarily remained the defining structures in our socio-economic, legal, and even political systems. Here are instances where contracts and transactions are useful:

- They help to protect our assets and set the organizational boundaries;

3

- They define and validate identities and chronicle all events;
- They can govern interactions among individuals, organizations, communities, and countries; and
- They can guide managerial and social actions.

In the recent past, these crucial tools and the bureaucracies formed to control them did not keep up with the fast-paced digital transformation due to centralization. Even though the centralization model consolidates the entire organization's contracts and transaction into a single database, it has led to inefficiencies such as:

- Increased monopolization;
- Top-level hierarchy in companies;
- Stagnation of firms;
- Obfuscation of firms; and
- Increased vulnerability to attacks.

If you consider how contemporary businesses work, you'll appreciate that maintaining the ongoing records is at the core of every company. These records must trace past actions and performance and guide firms to plan for the future. Essentially, records provide a view not only of how the company operates internally but also of its outside relationships.

At present, every company maintains its own records which are private. Many firms don't have a master ledger that keeps all their transactions. As such, their transactions are distributed across many internal units and functions. As a result, reconciling transactions across private and internal ledgers often take a lot of time and is prone to errors.

In most cases, failures of centralized networks have

triggered increased blanket legislation and regulation from government authorities. In the meanwhile, the original challenge remains: "How can these isolated ledgers communicate with other ledgers in an organization?"

Blockchain promises to solve this challenge.

So, what is Blockchain?

A Blockchain is simply a P2P (peer-to-peer) decentralized ledger or database.

Unlike the traditional ledger or database systems like SQL Server, MySQL, and Oracle, Blockchain can be shared, copied and synchronized among the computers—simply called nodes—in a network. Just like the traditional databases, Blockchain can record transactions and contracts such as transfer of data or assets among the computers in the network.

Blockchain was unveiled in 2008 as a proposal for Bitcoin—the first P2P, decentralized virtual currency—that eliminates centralized authorities about printing currency, transferring coins and validating transactions. In a sense, Bitcoin is the first application of the Blockchain technology.

The nodes in the network agree on valid transactions using consensus, and every transaction has a time stamp and unique cryptographic signature. All verified and validated records are placed on blocks which are linked and chained from the start of the chain to the most recent block, thus the name Blockchain.

As a result of consensus and cryptographic signatures,

Blockchain can provide an auditable history of all records without involving centralized or third parties such as clearing houses or financial institutions.

How Blockchain works

When you create a new transaction, or you want to modify an existing transaction, the transaction is broadcasted to the P2P network. When transmitted, a majority of the nodes on the Blockchain execute consensus algorithms that evaluate and validate the history of the individual block which has been proposed.

If the majority of the nodes agrees that the signature and history of the block is valid, then the new transaction is immutably written to the ledger, and a new block is appended to the Blockchain. On the other hand, if the majority of nodes don't agree, then the transaction or modification is denied, and a new block will not be appended to the chain.

The diagram below summarizes the mechanics of how Blockchain works:

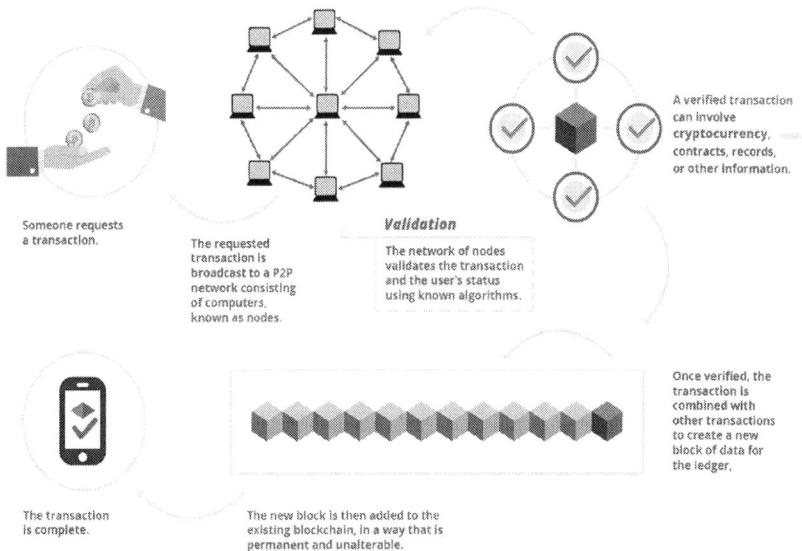

Someone requests a transaction.

The requested transaction is broadcast to a P2P network consisting of computers, known as nodes.

Validation

The network of nodes validates the transaction and the user's status using known algorithms.

A verified transaction can involve **cryptocurrency**, contracts, records, or other information.

Once verified, the transaction is combined with other transactions to create a new block of data for the ledger.

The transaction is complete.

The new block is then added to the existing blockchain, in a way that is permanent and unalterable.

Source: Blockgeeks.com

Now that you understand how Blockchain works let's unpackage the building blocks of Blockchain.

Cryptography and Blockchain

Blockchain technology is based on public-key cryptography. To understand the mechanics of public-key cryptography, let's first explain how symmetric or private-key cryptography it works.

Suppose Bob has a box with a lock. Usually, such as lock will have a key that can either lock or unlock the box. As such, if Bob wants to protect his belongings, he'll place them in the box and locks it. In such a case, only Bob or someone else that has Bob's copy of keys can unlock the box.

That's how private key cryptography works. You'll have

one key which you use it to encode ("lock") your data. If you want someone else to decode the box, you must share that key with him/her.

What about public-key cryptography?

Bob has a box. But this time, the box will have an exclusive lock. Instead of 2 states (locked and unlocked), the box will have 3 states (locked, unlocked and locked) in a counterclockwise direction. The box also has 2 separate keys (private, public). The first key will only turn clockwise (from lock to unlock to lock while the second one will turn counterclockwise (from lock to unlock to lock).

Bob picks the first key (private) and keeps it to himself. In this instance, the private key becomes his "secret" key since only Bob has it. The second key (public) becomes his "universal key." In fact, he can make hundreds of copies and give the public key to his friends.

Now, suppose Alice (one of Bob's friends) wants to send Bob a love letter.

Alice will place the document in the box and use a copy of Bob's public key to lock it. Since Bob's public key can only turn counterclockwise, it will lock the box. Once locked, no key apart from Bob's which can turn clockwise can unlock it. Since it's only Bob who has this key, he is the only one who can unlock it.

This is an example of public-key cryptography. The diagram below illustrates the concept further:

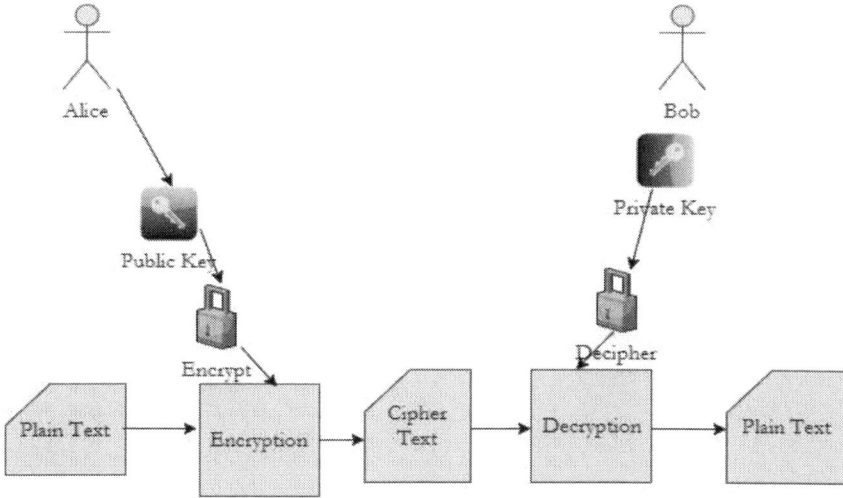

Public-key cryptography is an essential component of Blockchain as it ensures the integrity of transactions created by the protocol. The process of generating keys and signing of the transactions, which are key elements of any Blockchain platform heavily relies on public-key cryptography.

Whereas the public key in conjunction with a hash function generates a public address in the Blockchain, the private key is maintained secret and signs the digital transaction to ensure its origin is legitimate.

Suppose Alice wants to transfer some transactions to Bob.
Alice must first know her public and private keys that she will use to validate the transaction and identify herself to Bob. While the public key will be available to the whole world, her private key will be kept safe and secret. Obviously, the 2 keys generated must be related.

Besides, the 2 keys must be generated in a manner that

all users must know Alice's public key but not anyone (even Bob) should figure out her private key is he/she knows the public key. For the transaction to be validated on the Blockchain, Alice must sign the transaction with her private key to generate a digital signature. The digital signature helps to authenticate Alice's identity to Bob.

To create a digital signature, Alice will use both her private key and the transaction details such as the particulars of the car she's selling to Bob onto the Blockchain and create a hash function. The hash function will produce a fixed-size string as an output that is broadcasted to the Blockchain.

Formally, digital signatures depend on 2 basic functions:

```
Sign (Transactions, Private Key) -> Signature
Verify  (Message,  Public  Key,  Signature)  ->
True/False
```

In other words, given the transaction and a private key, the hash function generates a unique digital signature for the transaction. Given the transaction that we need to verify, its signature and the public key, the hash function generates a binary output depending on whether the signature is valid or not.

Once Alice signs the transaction, it is sent to the network where it awaits to be validated by miners. The miners will use Alice's public key (since they know it) to make sure the digital signature is valid in a consensus algorithm. This ensures the system is fool-proof. If the digital signature and ownership check out, the transaction is immutably recorded in the next block as follows:

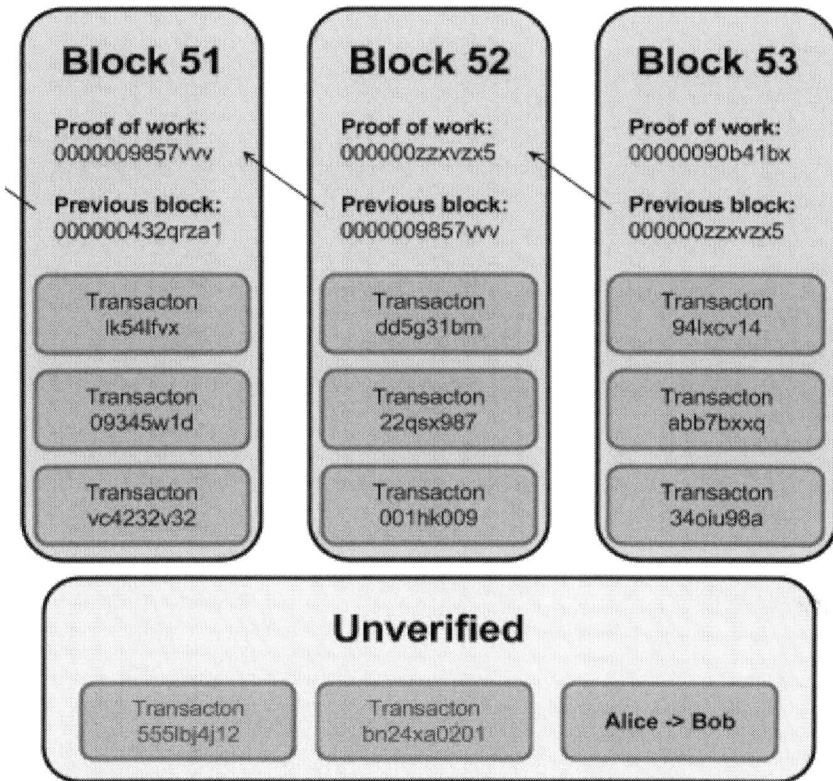

Block 51	Block 52	Block 53
Proof of work: 0000009857vvv	**Proof of work:** 000000zzxvzx5	**Proof of work:** 00000090b41bx
Previous block: 000000432qrza1	**Previous block:** 0000009857vvv	**Previous block:** 000000zzxvzx5
Transacton lk54lfvx	Transacton dd5g31bm	Transacton 94lxcv14
Transacton 09345w1d	Transacton 22qsx987	Transacton abb7bxxq
Transacton vc4232v32	Transacton 001hk009	Transacton 34oiu98a

Unverified

| Transacton 555lbj4j12 | Transacton bn24xa0201 | **Alice -> Bob** |

Source: Quora.com

I know you're thinking, "How are keys created?"

Private keys are randomly generated by the computing device whenever you request for a transaction on the Blockchain. In other words, Alice's PC or smartphone will generate a random private key the moment she requests for a transaction on the Blockchain.

However, her public key will be derived from the private key using the mathematical function that is based on Elliptic Curve Cryptography (ECC). Let me use an

11

illustration to explain how this mathematical function works:

Consider an elementary school pupil who has just mastered multiplication, but he/she is yet to learn division. Such a pupil may have learned from his teacher that the result of multiplying 3 by 4 is 12. To help him/her master multiplication, sometimes the teacher can hide 2 and display only 3 and 6 as follows:

To find the missing (?) number, the pupil may recall that his teacher once taught that 3*4=12, therefore fill in the missing number as 3. In other words, the pupil has multiplied his teacher's unique number (3) with 4 to obtain the result unaware that using division is simpler.

The same principle is applied in ECC.

Alice, who is initiating the transaction on the Blockchain will be gifted with both powers: multiplication and division. On the other hand, Bob and any user on the Blockchain will only use the multiplication powers. Because the private key that Alice will generate is a large number (this is not a problem with PCs), its corresponding public key won't be difficult on Alice's PC. This is because Alice's PC has both multiplication and division powers.

However, other public key holders will not be in a position to guess Alice's private key (as illustrated in the above example) because her key is a large prime number and they only have the multiplication powers.

Essentially, it's difficult to reverse-engineer the public key and obtain the private key.

Types of Blockchains

Blockchain can be categorized into 3 groups as follows:
- Permission-less Blockchains;
- Public Permissioned Blockchains; and
- Private Permissioned Blockchains

#1: Permission-less Blockchains

Under this category of Blockchains, no authority sanctions a transaction. Bitcoin and Ethereum are examples of permission-less Blockchains. You can think of permission-less Blockchains as shared public ledgers. For instance, if you send 5ETH to your friend, you are simply notifying all the people in the network.

All the nodes in the Ethereum network will get the transaction details and begin the process of validating the transaction where the node that verifies the transaction isn't chosen. Because no entity or person has control over validation of transactions, these Blockchains are used on platforms that want to be truly democratic.

#2: Public Permissioned Blockchains

In these Blockchains, there are chosen nodes that validate a transaction. For instance, validation can be performed by an authority, government, senior employees, institution or any person assigned and the public can access the data. For example, Alice may want to enhance transparency in Tilapia fish supply chain.

In such a case, Alice wants to customers to be confident about how the fish is caught, processed and even packaged. When a customer buys fish, he/she can scan the barcode and track the journey of the fish from the point it was caught. In other words, the customer is only viewing the data but doesn't have the permission to modify anything on the platform.

#3: Private Permissioned Blockchains
These Blockchains are similar to Public Permissioned Blockchain expect that the data isn't available for the public view. Suppose Alice's business involves 2 other small-scale companies which involve regular transactions with each other. In such a case, Alice's transactions with these 2 businesses are private and shouldn't be accessed by the public.

Popular Blockchains

Here are some popular Blockchains:
- **Ethereum**. It is a decentralized platform that runs smart contracts on a custom developed Blockchain.
- **HydraChain**. It is an Ethereum extension for developing permissioned distributed ledgers for private and other consortium chains.
- **BigChainDB**: It is an open source platform that adds Blockchain characteristics to Big Data distributed databases of immutability, decentralized control, and transfer of digital assets.
- **Chain Core**: It is Blockchain system that is used for issuing and transferring financial assets on a permissioned Blockchain platform.

- **Corda**: It is a distributed ledger platform that is used in pluggable consensus.
- **Credits**: It is a development framework for implementing permissioned decentralized ledgers.
- **Domus Tower Blockchain**: It is designed for regulated environments which are benchmarked at 1M transactions per second.
- **Elements Blockchain**: It is an open source, a protocol-level platform for extending the functionalities of Bitcoin.
- **Eris:db**. It is an open source, protocol level platform for extending the functionalities of Bitcoin.
- **Hyperledger Fabric**: It is a platform that supports the use of one or multiple networks for managing different assets, transactions and digital assets between the member nodes.
- **Hyperledger Iroha**. It is a modularized distributed ledger platform emphasis on mobile application development.
- **Hyperledger Sawtooth Lake**. It is a modular Blockchain suite where the transaction business logic is delinked from the consensus layer.
- **Multichain**. It is an open-source platform, based on the Bitcoin's Blockchain that can be applied to multi-asset financial transactions.
- **Openchain**: It is an open source distributed ledger platform for issuing and managing the digital assets.
- **Quorum**. It is an open source distributed database and smart contract system based on Ethereum.

15

- **Stellar.** It is an open-source, distributed payments system that uses the RESTful HTTP API servers to link to Stellar Core (the backbone of its network).

Now that we've explored the Blockchain technology in detail let's dig deeper to learn one of its applications: Ethereum and smart contracts.

Ethereum and smart contracts

Bitcoin was launched in 2013 to harness the power of Blockchain and transform the broken financial system. Because of the potency of Blockchain, Bitcoin has today matured into a trusted network for exchanging and storing value.

But Bitcoin is limited concerning the number of use cases it allows. For instance, "How can you negotiate a future economic contract or transaction using Bitcoin?"

Naturally, such a use case is impossible to achieve in Bitcoin.

Vitalik Buterin, a Russian-based programmer, and cryptocurrency researcher visualized things differently. He envisioned Ethereum as a "World Computer"—one that fits the description of a Virtual Machine. Combined with a Turing-complete language such as Solidity, a token (ETH) and gas (fuel), Vitalik envisioned a platform that would power every transaction on the network.

Inspired by Blockchain, Ethereum wasn't just competing to be "cash" but rather as a programmable system with mindboggling capabilities.

What is Ethereum?

Even though the terms Ethereum and Ether (ETH) are often used interchangeably, they don't mean the same thing. While Ethereum is a Blockchain platform upon which smart contracts are built, Ether is the cryptocurrency that fuels the Ethereum platform.

Ethereum was unveiled by Vitalik Buterin as a revolutionary platform for coding and running smart contracts and other Decentralized Apps (Dapps).

Example of a smart contract

Consider the illustration below:

Alice has given a contract of 100 ETH to Bob to implement a software system. Obviously, Alice will want the complete software to contain certain specifications. Instead of manually describing the specifications, she will hard-code all the conditions and requirements (functional, non-functional and domain) for the kind of software she wants on the Ethereum Blockchain.

Here is a simple diagrammatic illustration:

Alice   Bob

Smart Contract

Here, the Ethereum Blockchain assess the software that Bob will submit to ensure it has met all the conditions and specification specified by Alice. When the Ethereum

Blockchain indicates that all the specifications have been met, money will automatically be released to Bob.

On the other hand, if the specifications and conditions haven't been met, the code will be returned to Bob for revision. Here is how the process is handled in the smart contract:

- Bob submits his software on the Blockchain for verification;
- The system reviews the requirements;
- If the conditions have been met, the contract "self-executes" and 100ETH is transferred to Bob; and
- If the conditions and specification are not met, the code is returned to Bob for verification.

Here is the flow chart showing how the smart contract self-executes:

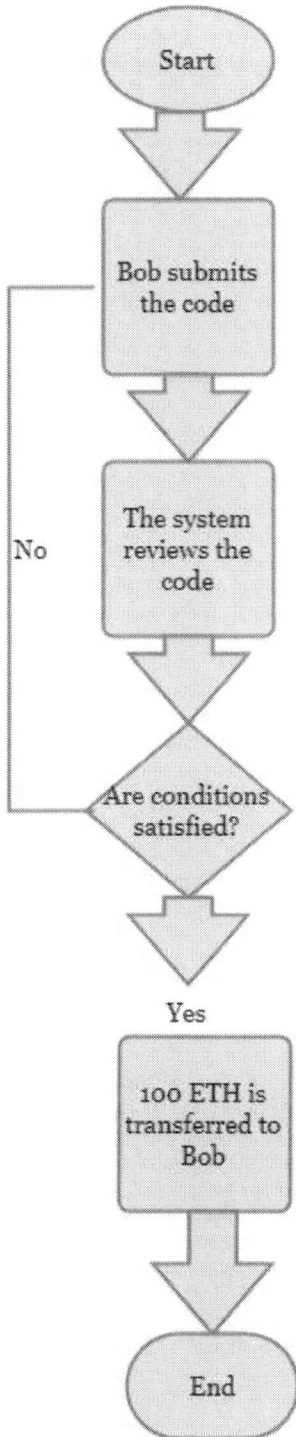

```
           ┌─────────────┐
           │    Start    │
           └─────────────┘
                  ↓
          ┌───────────────┐
          │  Bob submits  │
          │   the code    │
          └───────────────┘
                  ↓
          ┌───────────────┐
          │  The system   │
   No     │  reviews the  │
          │     code      │
          └───────────────┘
                  ↓
            ◇ Are conditions
              satisfied? ◇
                  ↓
                 Yes
          ┌───────────────┐
          │  100 ETH is   │
          │ transferred to│
          │      Bob      │
          └───────────────┘
                  ↓
           ┌─────────────┐
           │     End     │
           └─────────────┘
```

19

Note that Alice has no authority to stop the project until the requirement and conditions have been satisfied. Conversely, if the requirements haven't been met, then Bob must continue working on the project until he meets all the conditions.

From the discourse above, it is evident that Ethereum is more than just currency (ETH) that one can hold and invest in. It allows users to define and execute smart contracts that have enormous consequences.

So, what is a smart contract?

To solve all types of trust-related problems such as the one mentioned in the example above, the concept of "smart contract" emerged. A smart contract is simply a program that can self-execute when certain conditions in the system are met. Think of a smart contract as a particular type of account on the Blockchain.

Even though it's an account, it is not a typical account controlled by humans. A smart contract can be programmed to run all kinds of instructions like checking conditions, maintaining states and, obviously, receiving and transferring Ether. Because of the Blockchain's capability of immutability, the code on the Ethereum Blockchain can't be modified, or even hacked once it's coded.

Ethereum was created to be a platform where smart contracts are developed. Every time the smart contract runs, thousands of nodes or computers on the Blockchain execute the same contract. And every time the contract performs some action, all the nodes must agree that the action has actually taken place. This way, Ethereum acts a decentralized network allowing the smart contracts to run rather than relying on central authorities.

Whereas the Bitcoin protocol validates the ownership and transfer of bitcoins, the Ethereum platform validates the smart contracts and executes them according to encoded rules. Every account on the Blockchain will have a unique digital signature, which permits everyone to determine which account originated the transaction.

On a public Blockchain, any person can read/write data. While reading data is free, writing on the public blockchain isn't. You must pay to write on the Blockchain using a "gas" that is valued in Ether (ETH). The gaps help the network discourage spam and secure the protocol.

With its smart contracts capability, Ethereum hopes to be a massive decentralized computer—what is often called Ethereum Virtual Machine.

Differences between smart contracts and DApps

Smart contracts are codes which enforce agreements and execute themselves under specific conditions while DApps are a "Blockchain-enabled" websites. In other words, it's the smart contracts that allow the DApps to connect to the Blockchain. You can think of DApps as Ethereum-enabled websites while the smart contract is platforms that allow the DApps to connect to the Blockchain.

The straightforward way to understand the differences is mastering how conventional websites operate. Conventional sites are coded using HTML, CSS, and JavaScript to help render the page to users.

These websites may sometimes grab details using an API (Application Programming Interface) from a back-end database. For instance, when you log in to Twitter, the page calls an API to get your personal data and display them on the web page. Here is a sequence of actions:

Front-end $\rightarrow$ API $\rightarrow$ Back-end Database

A DApp is similar to a traditional website. Its front end uses the same technology when rendering the web page. However, instead of using an API to connect to the back-end database, a DApp uses a smart contract to connect to the Blockchain. Here is the flow chart:

Front-end $\rightarrow$ Smart Contract $\rightarrow$ Blockchain

Ethereum Virtual Machine

Ethereum implements smart contracts on the Blockchain using the Ethereum Virtual Machine (EVM). The EVM is simply an interpreter for the Ethereum's assembly language. As the interpreter executes, it maintains its stack and the memory byte-array. An instruction set on the Ethereum can look like this one:

```
PUSH1 0x90 PUSH1 0x70 MSTORE CALLVALUE IS ZERO
...
```

The EVM is limited when you compare it to other virtual machines. For instance, there is no way to perform input/output (IO) operations, make API (Application Programming Interface) calls or even generate random numbers. Ideally, the EVM can be regarded as a simple deterministic state machine.

As it' the case with assembly languages, writing programs is no fun. Therefore, high-level programming languages such as Solidity that can compile into EVM assembly have been developed.

Ethereum Technology stack
An Ethereum platform has a non-exhaustive list of elements with cryptographic tokens, the address system, consensus algorithms, miners/validators, the Blockchain ledger/database, Ethereum Virtual Machine (EVM), scripting language and complex economic structures.

The diagram below summarizes the Ethereum technology stack:

```
┌──────────────────────────────────────────────┐
│  ┌────────────────────────────────────────┐  │
│  │              Mist Browser              │  │
│  └────────────────────────────────────────┘  │
│                                                │
│  ┌────────────────────────────────────────┐  │
│  │                 DApps                  │  │
│  └────────────────────────────────────────┘  │
│                                                │
│  ┌──────────────┐ ┌──────────┐ ┌──────────┐  │
│  │Swarm (Storage)│ │ Whisper  │ │   EVM    │  │
│  │              │ │(Messaging)│ │(Consensus)│ │
│  └──────────────┘ └──────────┘ └──────────┘  │
│                                                │
│  ┌────────────────────────────────────────┐  │
│  │            Hardware Clients            │  │
│  └────────────────────────────────────────┘  │
│                                                │
│  ┌────────────────────────────────────────┐  │
│  │              The Internet              │  │
│  └────────────────────────────────────────┘  │
└──────────────────────────────────────────────┘
```

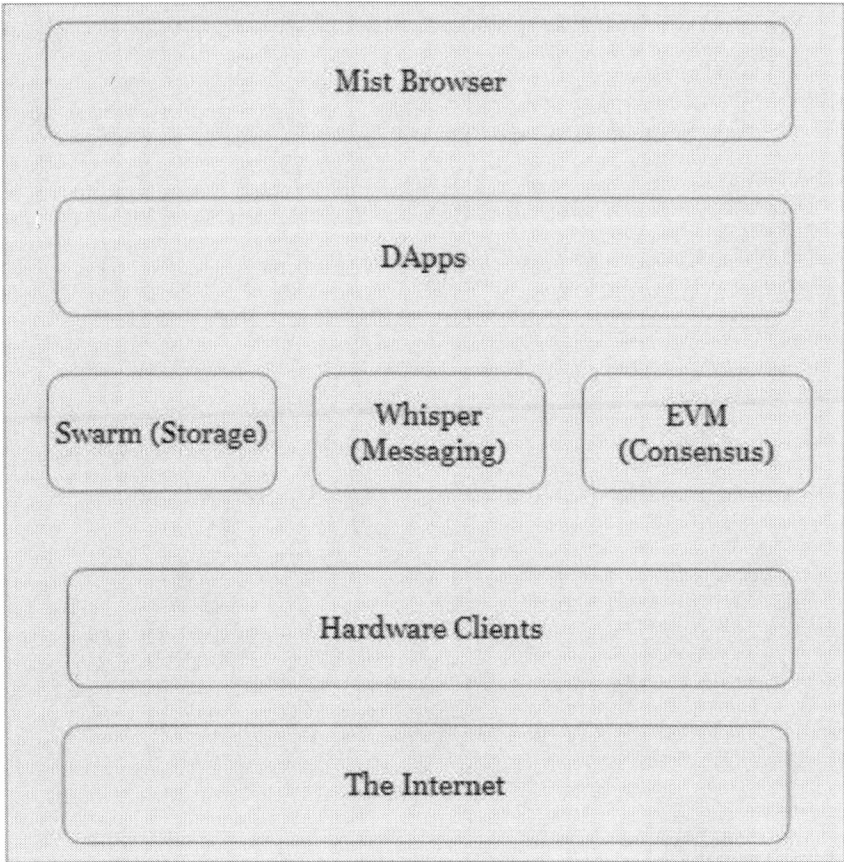

At the bottom of Ethereum stack is the Internet. Since Blockchain sits on top of the Internet, all the transactions and contracts defined on the Ethereum will be run on TCP/IP protocol.

Hardware clients sit on top of the Internet. For your hardware to support Ethereum, you will require a fast processing system with the following specifications:

- CPU: When choosing the CPU, you should go for a higher clock speed to deal with high-speed computations.

24

- RAM: At best, the minimum RAM capacity should be 4 GB.
- GPU: Ethereum computations are carried out within the GPU. Therefore, a robust GPU with high computational capabilities is required.
- Hard drive: You should go for SSD.

The third layer of the Ethereum stack technology comprises of software and their accompanying protocols. These rules support the growth and development of Ethereum by complementing the platform to execute more efficiently. Here are some of the supporting protocols:

- **Whisper**: It is a communications protocol and toolset that allows applications built on the Ethereum protocol stack to communicate to each other. It includes all the aspects of the distributed hash table and point-to-point communications platform to allow programs on the Ethereum platform to talk with one another.
- **Swarm (Swarm Hash)**: It is a P2P file sharing protocol that is used to efficiently store and retrieve data for use in the Ethereum programs and contracts. You can think of swarm as the BitTorrent for Ethereum.
- **EVM**: The EVM interprets the Ethereum's assembly language. As the interpreter executes, it maintains its stack and the memory byte-array.

The fourth layer of the Ethereum technology stack has Dapps. These are tools, programs, tools, or applications that execute on the Ethereum Blockchain.

At the top layer or the application layer of the Ethereum stack technology is the Mist. Mist provides users with capabilities to explore Dapps and offerings which utilize the Ethereum protocol. Unveiled as a distributed application discovery tool, Mist can act as a wallet for the smart contracts.

What are the various use cases for smart contracts?

Here are some smart contracts' use cases in different sectors:

#1: Banking

The smart contracts offer a single immutable ledger as the source of truth for data stored. Leveraging smart contracts in banking provides the banks with capabilities of automating clearing computations and approval workflows. This can eliminate costs, errors, and the inefficiency in payment settlements.

#2: Finance

Banking institutions can use smart contracts to offer a transparent and accurate recording of their fiscal data. Among the benefits that firms may accrue from transparency and accurate recordings include:

- Enhanced market stabilities;
- Reduced expenditure for storage of accounting systems via cost-sharing across many banking institutions; and
- Enhanced and better insights into the client's capital due to increased financial accessibility.

#3: Stock, Commodities, Option Trading

Smart contracts facilitate simplified and efficient international transfers of products and services via a faster letter of credit—which can be coded as a smart contract. Smart contracts that enhance financing automatically enables the payment approaches and the instruments of automation.

The benefits that accrue from using smart contracts in stock and commodities trading include:

- There are improved approval and payment initiations initiated by an automated letter of credit and contractual terms;
- There is enhanced efficiency about creation, validation, and modification of trade; and
- There is heightened the liquidity of financial assets.

#4: Supply chain management

Smart contracts can provide the required transparency and visibility that is necessary at every stage of a supply chain. IoT devices can add their agreements to the smart contract when the product is moved from the factory to the shelves in real-time. This can enhance the transparency of products movements. Here are some benefits of smart contracts in supply chain management:

- They simplify the delivery of complex multi-party systems;
- They strengthen supply chain financing and risk management through granular-level inventory tracking and delivery assurance;
- They reduce risks and fraud due to automated tracking and verification.

#5: Healthcare

Smart contracts can enhance clinical trials through improved cross-institutional research and visibility. As a result of improved sharing of patient data, smart contracts can offer the following benefits in healthcare:

- Enhanced visibility and reduced costs via streamlining of the setup processes in clinical trials;
- Increased access to the cross-institutionalized patient data in case there is an outbreak of epidemics. In this case, data is protected by the privacy-preserving algorithms in the smart contracts;
- Enhanced automation in obtaining and tracking consent for the shared access to patient data; and
- Increased confidence in privacy concerning sharing of patient data.

#6: Insurance

At present, the process of claiming from insurance firms in case of accidents is disjointed. These processes can be improved significantly via smart contracts. Essentially, the smart contract records the policy, driving records and even reports of drivers. With immutably stored data, IoT equipped vehicles can execute the initial claims in case there is an accident.

#7: E-commerce

Smart contracts can change all the processes involved in e-commerce. In the current scenario, a user orders goods and pay upfront for those goods to be delivered. Obviously, payment is made using the traditional payment gateway systems like PayPal and EFTs. These systems have high transactional costs that are paid in the form of merchant fee.

Besides, these systems take long periods for products and services to be delivered, and there is no way of tracking whether the product reached the buyer or not.

Smart contracts can serve as escrow services in the e-commerce platforms. As such, payment of goods and services will be withheld in the smart contract until the goods are actually delivered. The contract can only be fulfilled when payment has been released to the seller and products delivered to the buyer.

An example of an application that uses smart contracts is the Uber. The Uber platform system is executed via a smart contract where the contract begins the moment you agree to be picked up from your current location and be driven to another station. When all the requirements of the Uber transportation have been met, and you've been dropped at your destination, the contract is automatically triggered, and payment is completed for the service.

Summary

The aim of this chapter was to introduce you to Blockchain and smart contracts with a view to providing a background to Solidity programming. Therefore, we will introduce Solidity programming and tie it to smart contracts that have been explained in the previous sections. Let's get started.

Chapter 2: Introduction to Solidity

Ethereum would be incomplete today if there were no native language. Solidity is a language that allows Ethereum programmers to execute smart contracts on EVM. Even though it resembles the browser-based JavaScript language, Solidity can only execute Ethereum smart contracts.

In contrast to OOP languages like Java and JavaScript which combines variables, data, and functions to run specific human-operated commands, Solidity is a "contact-oriented" language. Its run-time environment tasks are all automated, and the objects are bundled together to eliminate manual commands.

Even though Solidity is often regarded as an Ethereum's scripting language, Solidity is a compiled language. It compiles smart contracts into bytecodes that the EVM can read and execute.

Lab Task

This task involves downloading Solidity IDE, configuring the Remix IDE and running a simple, smart contract. The Solidity versions adhere to semantic versioning and in addition to releases, has many developments builds. You should always use the latest release if you want better results.

Remix is an appropriate IDE to use if you want to learn

quickly how to code in Solidity by writing small contracts. To access Remix, launch your browser and point to http://remix.ethereum.org/.Here, you don't need to install anything since you are using an online version.

Overview of Remix

Remix is a suite of tools that can help you interact with the Ethereum Blockchain. When you point your browser to http://remix.ethereum.org/ here is what you see:

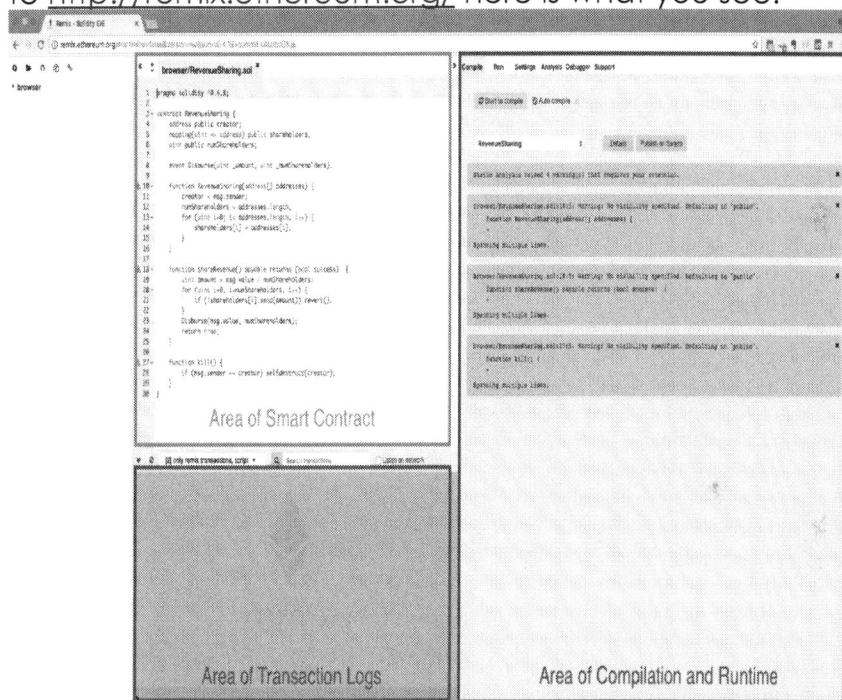

As you can see, the Remix screen is divided into several sections:

- ***Area for Smart Contract***: You'll be writing or copy/pasting the Solidity code in this section; and

- **Compilation and Runtime**: It will generate any compilation/runtime errors or warnings.
- **Transaction Logs**: All the transaction details will be observed in this section.

There are several tools inside the Remix framework. However, the following tools are of our utmost interest:

1. **Solidity Compiler**: It generates useful information about the compiled Solidity code that you can in other development environments; and
2. **Runtime Environment**: The Remix framework provides 3 runtime environments:
   - **Injected Web3**: It runs and deploys the smart contract on providers such as MetaMask or Mist
   - **Web3 Provider**: It runs smart contracts on localhost via IPC.
   - **JavaScript VM**: It is a simulated environment

The Remix editor recompiles the smart contract every time the current file is altered, or you chose another file. It also offers syntax highlighting that is automatically mapped to the Solidity keywords. If you want to use Remix without connecting to the Internet, launch your browser and go to https://github.com/ethereum/browser-solidity/tree/gh-pages where you will download a ".zip" file and follow the instructions explained on the web page to install it on your PC.

To quickly see how Remix compiles and executes smart contracts, copy/paste the following code into Remix window:

```
pragma solidity ^0.4.19;
contract helloworld {
    address namisiko;
    function helloworld() {
        namisiko = msg.sender;
    }
}
```

Now click the compile link followed by a run link to compile and execute the smart contract respectively. Here is what you should see the output:

```
====== helloworld.sol:helloworld ======

EVM assembly:

  mstore(0x40, 0x60)

  ... */ "helloworld.sol":25:125  contract helloworld {

  jumpi(tag_1, iszero(callvalue))

  invalid

tag_1:

tag_2:

...
```

As you can see, the output is just a long list of opcodes. Here is what you should note about the code that you've just typed:

The first line specifies the version of solidity that you're using. In our case, we are using Solidity version 0.4.19.

The second line "contract helloworld" defines the name of the contract that we are generating on the Blockchain. In this case, helloworld is the name of the contract. The name of the contract is opened just like a

JavaScript class as follows:

```
contract helloworld {
```

When you click on the Run tab, you will see a screen that appears as follows:

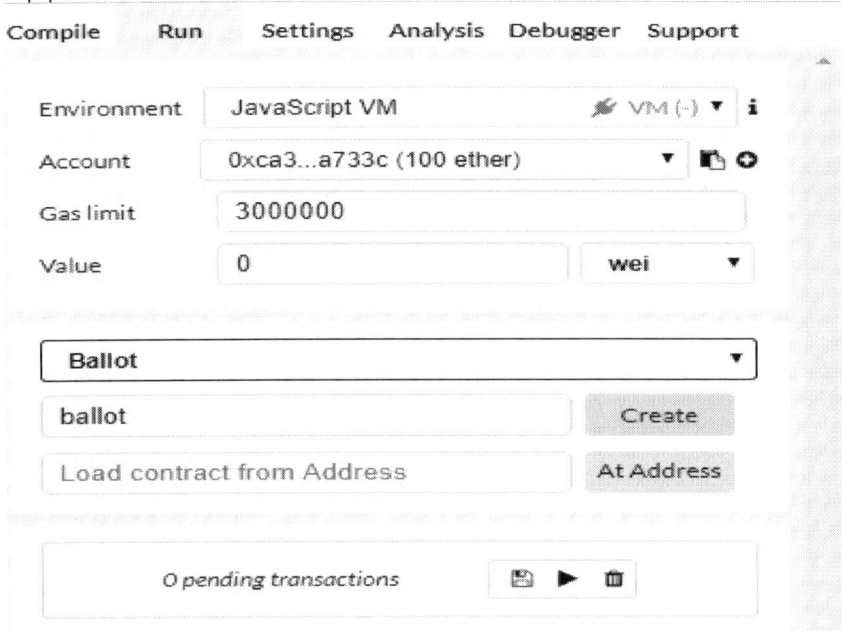

| Compile | Run | Settings | Analysis | Debugger | Support |

Environment	JavaScript VM	VM (-) ▼ ℹ
Account	0xca3...a733c (100 ether)	▼ 📋 ⊕
Gas limit	3000000	
Value	0	wei ▼

| Ballot ▼ |
| ballot | Create |
| Load contract from Address | At Address |

0 pending transactions   💾 ▶ 🗑

Smart contracts are executed just the same way JavaScript programs are executed. Therefore, we must have a JavaScript VM. That is what you see under the Environment label in the window. Similarly, smart contract resides at a given address on the Blockchain.

The information about the smart contract address is specified by the Account label. To check the address and other information, click on the Details button under Debugger Tab. You'll see something like this:

[vm] from:0xca3...a733c, to:▓▓▓▓▓▓▓▓▓▓▓▓▓▓▓▓▓(constructor), va **Details** Debug lue:0 wei, data:0x606...60029, 0 logs, hash:0x5ba...88d2a	
status	0x1 Transaction mined and execution succeed
contractAddress	0x692a70d2e424a56d2c6c27aa97d1a86395077b3a
from	0xca35b7d915458cf540adeG068dfe2f44c8fa733c
to	▓▓▓▓▓▓▓▓▓▓▓▓▓▓▓▓▓(constructor)
gas	3000000 gas
transaction cost	68653 gas
execution cost	10661 gas
hash	0x5ba15059166da60b140e2cca3ad917b697fb6aeaa63b1e6cb7a9ba5437a88d2a
input	0x60606040523415600e57600080fd5b603500601b6000396000f300606060401052600080fd00a16 5627a7a7230582048f3ce53cd41bb0972a8989feda+04d182e3caa72ad368b0e53d63aa89aa4716002 9
decoded input	{}
decoded output	-
logs	[]
value	0 wei

Every time a smart contract is executed, nodes on the Ethereum Blockchain must validate the contract through consensus mining. As you can see from the screen above, the gas specified is 3000000. Think of gas as the execution fee that you will use to send your transactions for verification on the Ethereum network.

Types of variables in Solidity

In Solidity, you'll specify a variable by defining its type. The table below summarizes the variables in Solidity:

Variable	Description
bool	Boolean: It returns true or false.
int / uint	Integer/Unsigned Integers: They represent integers or numeric values. The main difference between int and uint is that int can hold negative

35

	numbers as values while `uint` cannot.
address	Address: The address type represents a 20-byte value, which is meant to store the Ethereum address on the Blockchain. Variables that are typed as address also have members, comprising of balances and transfers.
bytes1 through 32	bytes1 through to 32: This is a fixed-size byte array.
bytes	A dynamically-sized array
string	A dynamically-sized string
mapping	Hash tables that have key types and value types.
structs	They allow programmers to define new types

Visibility of variables

Solidity has 4 categories of visibilities for both the variables and functions:

- Public: Public variables and function allow you to specify functions or variables which can be called internally or via messages.
- Private: Private variables and functions are only local to the current contract and not any derived contracts.
- Internal Functions: These are functions and variables that can only be accessed locally.
- External Functions: These functions can be called from other smart contracts and transactions.

Smart contract constructors

Every smart contract that you will create must a

constructor function. The constructor is called whenever a contract is generated. Inside the constructor, you can specify the values of variables.
Consider the code below:

```
pragma solidity ^0.4.19;
contract Employees {
   string f_name;
   uint age;
   function setEmployees(string _fname, uint _age)
public {
      f_name = _fname;
      age = _age;
   }
     function  getEmployees()  public  constant
returns (string, uint) {
      return (f_name, age);
   }
}
```

As you can see, we have 2 functions, setEmployees () and getEmployees (). The function setEmployees accepts 2 arguments, _fname and _age. When it's called, it sets the string f_name to the returned _fname and does the same with age.

On the other hand, the getEmployees () function has been defined as a constant, and it returns a string and a uint. This is where f_name is returned and age variable once the function is called. Now, click on the create button and under "setEmployees" button, type: "Namisiko Enterprises," 34 and hit the button.

Next, click on the getEmployees () button and notice how it returns the inputted value! This is how you'll be setting variables from user input in any smart contract.

Lab challenge

Launch your browser and point it to http://www.remix.org. Now type the following code and compile it in Remix Editor:

```
pragma solidity ^0.4.19;
contract BoardVotes {
   string titles;
   string descs;
   function castVote(string _title, string desc)
public {
      titles = _title;
      descs = description;
   }
   function getPublics() public constant returns
(string, uint) {
      return;
   }
   }
}
```

Note what happens when you run it and deploy it. What happens when you change the URL of Remix Editor to https://www.remix.org?

Summary

This chapter has explored Blockchain and Ethereum to provide a big-picture view of solidity programming. Some of the important concepts that we have examined are:

- **Blockchain**: A Blockchain is a P2P (peer-to-peer) decentralized ledger or database. Blockchain was unveiled in 2008 as a proposal for Bitcoin—the first P2P, decentralized virtual currency—that eliminates centralized authorities about printing currency, transferring coins and validating transactions. In a sense, Bitcoin is the first application of the Blockchain technology. Blockchain can be categorized as either Permission-less, Public Permissioned Blockchains; or Private Permissioned Blockchains.

- **Smart contracts**: A smart contract is a program that can self-execute when specific conditions in the system are met. A smart contract can be programmed to run all kinds of instructions like checking conditions, maintaining states and, obviously, receiving and transferring Ether. Because of the Blockchain's capability of immutability, the code on the Ethereum Blockchain can't be modified, or even hacked once it's coded. Ethereum was created to be a platform where smart contracts are developed.

- **DApps**: Whereas DApps as Ethereum-enabled websites, the smart contract is platforms that allow the DApps to connect to the Blockchain.

- **Solidity**: Solidity is a language that allows Ethereum programmers to execute smart contracts on EVM. Even though it resembles the browser-based JavaScript language, Solidity can only execute Ethereum smart contracts. Its run-time environment tasks are all automated, and the objects are bundled together to eliminate manual commands.

References

1. https://www.techspot.com/article/1567-blockchain-explained/
2. https://www.dataforeningen.no/getfile.php/393706 2.1488.ftfbuwpqqb/Krogdahl_Pal_Blockchain+Explained.pdf
3. https://www.coindesk.com/information/ethereum-smart-contracts-work/
4. http://www.primechaintech.com/docs/blockchain/ Nuts%20and%20bolts%20of%20Blockchain.pdf
5. https://blockgeeks.com/guides/smart-contracts/
6. https://www.coindesk.com/information/how-ethereum-works/
7. https://www.ibm.com/blockchain/what-is-blockchain.html
8. https://www.quora.com/blockchains
9. http://solidity.readthedocs.io/en/v0.4.21/types.html
10. http://solidity.readthedocs.io/en/v0.4.21/installing-solidity.html

http://remix.readthedocs.io/en/latest/

Chapter 3: Smart Contracts with Web3.Js

Prerequisites

In this chapter, several programming assignments in Web3.Js will be introduced. No prior experience with Web3.Js is required. However, elementary programming language or prior experience with programming languages such as JavaScript or Python is essential. In addition, you'll be required to have a basic understanding of the following concepts:

- Blockchain and smart contracts(covered in chapter 1);
- Programming in Solidity;
- Linux commands; and
- Basic Linux administration skills

Theory

Basic terminologies used in DApps programming

It's important to differentiate between levels of the Ethereum stack to help you create a clear idea of each part's mechanics and roles. This way, you'll avoid getting lost in the speculation and begin to see where your apps are utilizing the stack. Here are some terminologies that you must be familiar with before getting started with Web3.Js:

1. *Web3*

41

It is the next generation worldwide web. Web3 has been adopted by the Ethereum platform and co-opted to refer to a decentralized Internet. In other words, Web3 is just Web2 (the current web) but without centralized servers and isolated data silos.

If everything goes according to plan, Web3 is primed to become part of the Internet and Web3 developers will become Web developers. In time, the decentralized architecture provided by Ethereum platform will become an infrastructure of choice, just like MongoDB verses Firebase or REST verses GraphQL is today.

Even though the changeover may be gradual, on Web 2.0, we're increasingly seeing websites whose back-ends utilize Web 3.0-like elements like Bitcoin, BitTorrent, and NameCoin. This trend is set to continue and a truly Web-3.0 platform Ethereum will likely be used by websites that wish to offer transactional evidence of their content such as exchanges and exchanges.

2. DApp

A DApp is a decentralized application. If you're old school web developer, a DApp is just a website that has no server. Rather its "backend" code executes on a decentralized P2P (peer-to-peer) network of computers (nodes) and the "frontend" code is served from a distributed Content Delivery Network (CDN). The diagram below summarizes DApp mechanics:

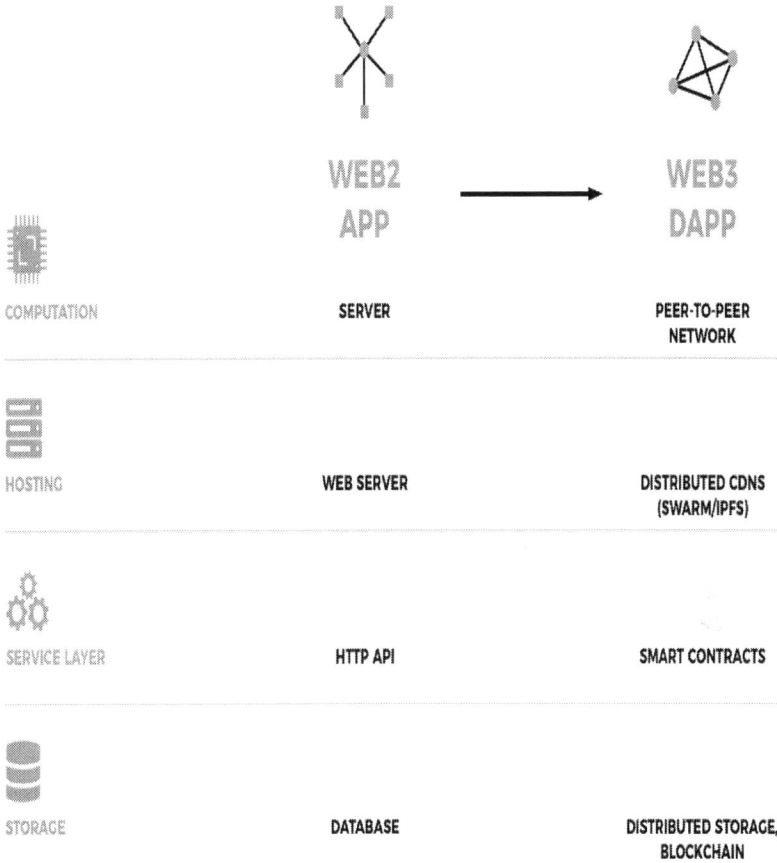

	WEB2 APP	WEB3 DAPP
COMPUTATION	SERVER	PEER-TO-PEER NETWORK
HOSTING	WEB SERVER	DISTRIBUTED CDNS (SWARM/IPFS)
SERVICE LAYER	HTTP API	SMART CONTRACTS
STORAGE	DATABASE	DISTRIBUTED STORAGE, BLOCKCHAIN

Source: Hackernoon.com

3. Blockchain

Think of Blockchain as an add-only database that, which instead of being stored on a single server, is distributed among many nodes that each keep the entire transaction history of the network. Blockchain stores data in an immutable form to create a chain of data packets (transactions) which have a set of operations that documents some particular activity.

43

For instance, in Bitcoin, the transactions stored are purely financial in nature (Alice sent Bob x bitcoins). In Ethereum, you can run a variety of transaction types by using smart contracts which have rules for processing the transactions.

4. Ethereum

Ethereum is a distributed computing platform that leverages Blockchain to provide scripting functionality via smart contracts. DApps can use Ethereum and its associated technologies that is the focus of this book.
Now that you have a basic understanding of terminologies in DApps programming, let's dive in and explore various development platforms.

Development platforms

To interact with the Ethereum Blockchain, you must use various platforms. These libraries are developed for a particular language and programming protocol. Here are some of the most common platforms that you'll require:

- Web3.Js;
- EthereumJs modules; and
- PyEVM

Besides the above 3 frameworks, you can also use various tools. The table below summarizes the various frameworks that are in use:

Client	Language	Developers

PyEVM	Python	Ethereum Foundation/Piper Meriam
Ethereum(J)	Java	Ether.Camp
Parity	Rust	Ethcore
CPP-Ethereum	C++	Ethereum Foundation
go-ethereum	Golang	Ethereum Foundation
Quorum (Private and permissioned client)	Go (Forking the go-ethereum)	JP Morgan
Ethereum modules	JavaScript	Ethereum Foundation

EthereumJs libraries are used to sign and execute raw transactions. Essentially, the EthereumJs community creates JavaScript tools that implement the core Ethereum platforms, APIs, and protocols to help developers seamlessly interact with the Ethereum Blockchain and implement their own DApps.

On the other hand, PyEVM is the Python core library for implementing the Ethereum smart contracts. It offers basic classes and appropriate routines for interacting with the smartcontracts. The virtual machine contains all the necessary software that can help you code any smartcontract that interacts with the Blockchain.

Today, PyEVM has been implemented as either CPP-Ethereum—C++ implementation— and Go-Ethereum (Geth).

Let's now turn to Web3.Js because it is the most popular among the libraries.

Overview of Web3.Js

Web3.Js is Ethereum-compatible JavaScript API and implements the Generic JSON RPC (Remote Procedure Calls) specification. These libraries are available on npm (node package manager) as a node module. If you're using a browser, and its related components, you can find these libraries embedded in JavaScript and will also be bundled in the meteor.Js package.

Web3.Js communicates through RPC with the local nodes or test nodes on the Blockchain. To help you fast-track creating scripts, development environments like Truffle can help you access the Web3.Js libraries quickly. When a Solidity-coded smart contract has been compiled using solc and transmitted to the Blockchain, you can call it using Ethereum Web3.Js API and create DApps that interact with contracts.

Web3.Js contains the following objects:
- Eth object (Web3.eth): It is used for creating Ethereum Blockchain interactions; and
- Shh object (Web3.shh): It is used for Whisper interaction;
- Bzz object (web3.bzz): It is used for the swarm protocol which is a decentralized file storage protocol; and
- Utils object (Web3.util): It contains helper functions for DApp programmers.

Getting started with Web3.Js

To get started with Web3.Js, you must first get the framework into your project. There are 3 methods:

- Using the npm approach: Here is the code that you can use to get Web3.Js into your DApp project:

```
npm install web3
```

- Using the meteor approach: Here is the code that can help you install Web3.Js:

```
meteor add ethereum:web3
```

- Using the pure js approach: Here you can link your project to `dist/web3.min.js`

After that importing Web3.Js, you'll need to create a web3 instance and set the provider. The Ethereum supported browsers such as MetaMask or Mist have an ethereumProvider or the web3.currentProvider that can help you get started. For Web3.Js, check web3.givenProvider. If the property is null, then you should link to a remote or local node to use Web3.

To help you integrate Web3 into different types of projects with unique standards, there are multiple approaches that can act on the asynchronous functionalities. However, the majority of Web3.Js objects employ callback as the last argument, as well as returning the promises to Blockchain functions.

As a Blockchain, Ethereum has various levels of finality and therefore should return multiple phases of an action. To cope with regulations and requirements, you'll have to return a "promiEvent" for functions such as

47

web3.eth.sendTransaction or contract methods.

The "promiEvent" is a promise that has been combined with an event emitter to act on different phases of actions on the Blockchain, such as a transaction. PromiEvents work just like normal promises but with added on.once and off functionalities.

This way, you can watch for additional events such as "receipt" or "transactionHash." Here is the code illustration:

```
web3.eth.sendTransaction    ({from:    '0x132...',
data: '0x421...'})
.once ('transactionHash', function (hash) {...})
.once('receipt',        function(receipt){    ...
}).on('confirmation',    function    (confNumber,
receipt){ ... })
.on ('error', function (error) { ... })
.then (function (receipt){
// the transactions in this section will be fired
once the receipt has been mined
});
```

Json interface

The Json interface is an object that describes the ABI (Application Binary Interface) for the Ethereum smart contract. Using Json interface with Web3.Js can help you create JavaScript object that represents the smart contract together with its methods and events using the Web3.eth.Contract object as follows:

```
contract Smart_Test {
uint a;
address d = 0x12367890123456789012343456789012;
function
Testing(uint testInt)   { a = testInt;}
event Events(uint indexed b, bytes32 c);
```

```
event Events2(uint indexed b, bytes32 c);
function
Test2(uint b, bytes32 c) returns(address) {
Events(b, c);
return
d;
}
}
```

Aim

In the last chapter, we explored the theory behind Blockchain and smart contracts. We also introduced you to Solidity—the scripting language behind Ethereum smart contracts. Specifically, we learned how you could download Remix IDE, configure it and use to code your smart contracts.

In this chapter, we will learn how to use the Ethereum ganache-cli—a replacement of TestRPC—and Web3.Js to help you create a basic user interface for connecting to Ethereum smart contract. Let's dive in.

Lab Activity

In this lab session we will require the following tools:
- Ganache-cli;
- Web3.Js; and
- Remix IDE

Here is the workflow that we'll use:

Ethereum Solidity and Ganache-cli

Install Web3.Js

Configure and update Remix IDE

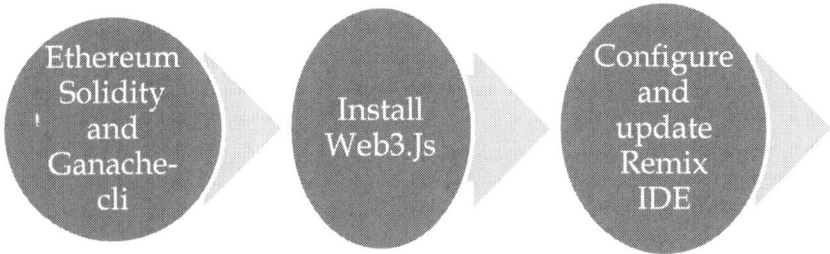

Installation

Getting started with Ethereum and Solidity programming on Windows platforms can be tedious for most developers because most Solidity tools are designed for Linux systems. If you're already using Linux, you should have no problem. However, if you're using Windows the easiest way to start using Solidity and its related frameworks is to use the Linux subsystem feature that has recently been introduced in Windows 10.

If you're using the previous version, I recommend upgrading them to Windows 10. With the Linux subsystem tool, you can execute Ubuntu (including its Bash shell) on Windows platforms, without dual-booting your PC. It also uses minimal resources than if you're using a virtual machine.

Proceed as follows:
- Ensure that you are running a 64-bit Windows on your PC
- Modify your PC to support the "Developer Mode" if it has not been enabled. Go to Settings and click

50

on "Update and Security." Here is what you should see:

For developers

Use developer features

These settings are intended for development use only.

Learn more

○ Windows Store apps

Only install apps from the Windows Store.

○ Sideload apps

Install apps from other sources that you trust, like your workplace.

◉ Developer mode

Install any signed and trusted app and use advanced development features.

- Under the "For Developers" tab, enable the "Developer mode" and wait for it to be activated.
- Now, go to the Windows Features by clicking Settings>Windows Features>Turn Windows features on or off. In the window that appears, enable the "Windows Subsystem for Linux."

Windows Features   —   □   ×

Turn Windows features on or off

To turn a feature on, select its check box. To turn a feature off, clear its check box. A filled box means that only part of the feature is turned on.

- [ ] RIP Listener
- [ ] ⊞ Simple Network Management Protocol (SNMP)
- [ ] Simple TCPIP services (i.e. echo, daytime etc)
- [×] ⊞ SMB 1.0/CIFS File Sharing Support
- [ ] Telnet Client
- [ ] TFTP Client
- [ ] Windows Identity Foundation 3.5
- [×] ⊞ Windows PowerShell 2.0
- [ ] ⊞ Windows Process Activation Service
- [×] Windows Subsystem for Linux
- [ ] Windows TIFF IFilter
- [×] Work Folders Client
- [×] XPS Viewer

OK   Cancel

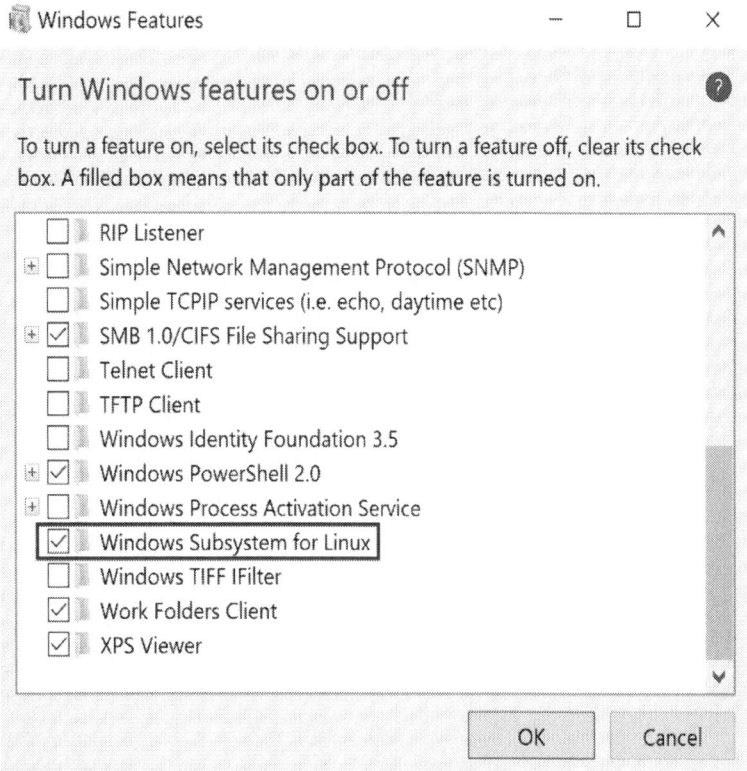

- Wait for it to install the required files and restart your PC. If your PC reboots, you will now be able to access the Bash Terminal from the Start menu by just typing "bash" in the search box.
- Launch the Bash Terminal from the start menu by typing "bash" in the search box. This will prompt you to download Ubuntu for your system. Follow the onscreen instructions to complete installing Ubuntu on your PC.
- Once Ubuntu has been installed, it's now time to begin installing Solidity and frameworks.
- Now, launch the Bash Terminal and type the following command to update the OS:

```
sudo apt-get update
```

Here is what you should see:

- Now install the curl libraries by typing the following command:

```
sudo apt-get install curl
```

- Next, we install nvm—node version manager— which we shall be using to install the NodeJS. It also bundles the npm (node package manager) for NodeJS. Type the following command at the command prompt and hit the Enter key:

```
curl                                        -o-
https://raw.githubusercontent.com/creationi
x/nvm/v0.33.0/install.sh | bash
```

53

Here is what you should get:

```
Keisha@Oddillia:~$ sudo apt-get install curl
Reading package lists... Done
Building dependency tree
Reading state information... Done
curl is already the newest version (7.47.0-1ubuntu2.7).
The following package was automatically installed and is no longer required:
  libfreetype6
Use 'sudo apt autoremove' to remove it.
0 upgraded, 0 newly installed, 0 to remove and 122 not upgraded.
Keisha@Oddillia:~$ ▪
```

- To check the version of your `nvm`, simply type:

```
nvm --version
```

- Now, install the NodeJS by running the `nvm` command as follows:

```
nvm install node
```

- Set it up for use in your Bash shell as follows:

```
nvm use node
```

- Next, install the solc (Solidity compiler) by using `npm` as follows:

```
npm install -g solc
```

Now is the time to install the Ganache (formerly called TestRPC). Ganache is an emulator that will enable you to test your smart contracts on the Blockchain and work on their implementation without the associated overheads of deploying them on a public Blockchain. In a sense, Ganache provides you a virtual Blockchain platform where you can code, test, and debug out all the errors in the smart contract before deploying them to a public Blockchain.

- Type the following command at the command prompt and hit the Enter key:

```
npm install -g truffle
```

Here is what you'll get:

- Next, install the Ganache command line interface by typing the command below:

```
npm install -g ganache-cli
```

Here is what you should see:

- Now launch another Bash shell and confirm that Ganache is working. Type the following command at the command prompt and hit the Enter key:

```
ganache-cli
```

Here is what I got:

```
Keisha@Oddillia:~$ ganache-cli
Ganache CLI v6.1.0 (ganache-core: 2.1.0)

Available Accounts
==================
(0) 0x8e98ab719fb1a29ac6d9581c154834f9f1fba014
(1) 0xe6677799176f9bff181633a919c8ce05f0db9d8f
(2) 0xf6c9430cde0bd98425ad0eda3d5634befc285ab0
(3) 0x945977dd2cea80c33200cfb01703257be3b54603
(4) 0xda8d2d850c140bd0215bee25de766d97557b5f24
(5) 0x093a9a24ea18e119c19b350852c72b157d6c76a4
(6) 0x6b5a7f3c4c1fd8ecbf66b7f11609fdbe54875484
(7) 0x72499356a9eb9bb08b25f585f60ee475883aa39f
(8) 0x191ca3c275679f2d5f094e6460fef5a093c08d39
(9) 0x68160109b32b3d5999c270bdf19b8c5ed8ea1391

Private Keys
==================
(0) 8285307e0651a979194762877246a1104d0427f2ea47a2e48b60e1f28911f227
(1) 6085eb0c9fafad58805d12b714f132ffa35e3fa562cc891dce724291215a88eb
(2) 086d2ddc43a1da951297d2989d6fb4cf786bd45938a47be928f2148049a754c0
(3) a13219634b47d37a0643f254386f7e8d664249e2a5be33acf4c8261d8aefb32c
(4) f905e6ead7356d3866ff348082e5b95dd95464c4ca9e3ece5934491b9f134f5a
(5) 8d249afbccb36d0d1f8f5db23bb91f6fb68c9c7158186b06d8c5631e74be37bc
(6) 5cc508b6addf729d5553f69215d6655573215a39bb5ee092a8e012205d5b1379
(7) 11dd7041ef94053218e140651bef31fd8a011d636ff480caba8720347a0d5c60
(8) 362784ea6841cd72479dd4419078dc8cbecefe023ab83f3779449a151a5b9ca8
(9) 33f3527d6d3ee4405bfa9d04fa7d76123c90493b4b58bd7ce6bcf11421a13f74

HD Wallet
==================
Mnemonic:      subway trip water monitor chalk parade source call wrap mimic direct develop
Base HD Path:  m/44'/60'/0'/0/{account index}
```

As you can see, Ganache displays available accounts and their corresponding private keys that are followed by a notification which displays *"Listening on localhost: 8545…"*

Next, we install Web3.Js.

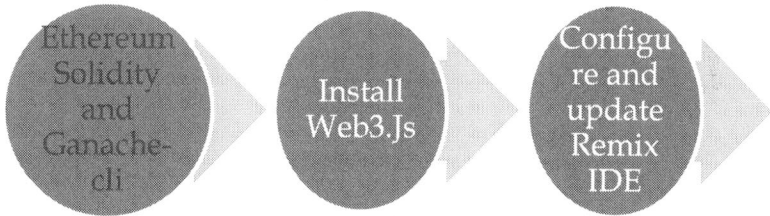

Installing Web3.Js

- Before you install Web3.Js, it is important to create its own folder in a new console window. Proceed as follows to create the folder. Navigate to /home and type the following commands:

```
cd /home/Keisha
mkdir Solidity
```

- Launch the Bash Terminal and type the following command:

```
npm install web3
```

Here is what I got:

```
make: Entering directory '/home/Keisha/node_modules/websocket/build'
  CXX(target) Release/obj.target/bufferutil/src/bufferutil.o
  SOLINK_MODULE(target) Release/obj.target/bufferutil.node
  COPY Release/bufferutil.node
  CXX(target) Release/obj.target/validation/src/validation.o
  SOLINK_MODULE(target) Release/obj.target/validation.node
  COPY Release/validation.node
make: Leaving directory '/home/Keisha/node_modules/websocket/build'
npm WARN saveError ENOENT: no such file or directory, open '/home/Keisha/package.json'
npm      created a lockfile as package-lock.json. You should commit this file.
npm WARN enoent ENOENT: no such file or directory, open '/home/Keisha/package.json'
npm WARN Keisha No description
npm WARN Keisha No repository field.
npm WARN Keisha No README data
npm WARN Keisha No license field.

+ web3@1.0.0-beta.33
added 7 packages and moved 1 package in 148.71s
Keisha@Oddillia:~/Solidity$
```

- Next, configure the Remix IDE so that you start coding in Web3.Js.

Remix IDE configuration

Here is how you can configure the Remix IDE:

- Switch over to the Remix IDE by launching your browser and pointing it to http://remix.ethereum.org/
- Click on the Run link, and then alter the Environment's dropdown from JavaScript VM to Web3 Provider.
- Follow the onscreen instructions to change the environment.
- Click the "OK" button and specify the Ganache localhost address. By default, the Ganache's address is http://localhost:8545.

What we have just performed above is changing the deployment environment. Instead of using JavaScript VM, you will now be using the Ganache client on your PC. You can now execute any code in Web3.Js by simply typing the smart contract on the Remix' Editor.

Just as we executed a simple contract in the previous chapter, type the following code in the Remix's Editor and click on Run>Create.

```
pragma solidity ^0.4.19;
```

```
contract BoardVotes {
    string titles;
    string descs;
    function castVote(string _title, string desc)
public {
        titles = _title;
        descs = description;
    }
    function getPublics() public constant returns
(string, uint) {
        return;
    }
}
}
```

Start Ganache

Launch the Bash Terminal and split the screen into 2. You can use either `tmux` or `screen` apps to help you split the screen. We shall use the left-hand side of the screen to execute `node consoles` while the right-hand side will handle the ganache-cli. On the right-hand side of the Terminal, type the following command to start ganache-cli:

```
ganache-cli
```

Here is what I have:

```
Keisha@Oddillia:~$
```

```
====================
(0) 0x921a565d59bbc5bafc6337e252ec9228fd2318e2
(1) 0x20b8ecd135e6abf57d7bd0baf884ca81006a6924
(2) 0xa901959b4b692fdbde5b17c05fb7a929869ee345
(3) 0xf294f6b1a2e6ba047dedaa57f1eae6fbc3884cfc
(4) 0x4e7a26b69f6b1c59a119e79599ea1bd75022f5f4
(5) 0x86d975b09a3cde468f9feb79e3eaccbd9b108b72
(6) 0x0d7e2691407ee005db8a9f8284a91c7c66a37ad9
(7) 0xef050cebaf4ea135488db1bec53f3d60213e162f
(8) 0xde3aec1a698a76fe3fbd99c215e3f8942656c18b
(9) 0xa8ce7144f539faf8e02f486d18782637313b06c2

Private Keys
====================
(0) f209ef5aadedf62fe81011293ee08b577484bebfa49a603156ef4e96bb7b55ec
(1) a94fa06127b6572e4eb04dfb18acac5212d22b0e11960527b069597c730092b2
(2) 4b1260f92d4b1cec8c2ee65afe2cf2221e604921160abb19c13d289501Ba2970
(3) 73292a6a22cb225256ee1c441a730388850d77ad674934e6933196050c9432a7
(4) 7cd43493e2b355e51ad702bcd7da2d1a7bd849083a276522e87b8d2bf88ab350
(5) 310e504dce7fa662453ef02d950ead15c95a2171b70f90187ef13bfd4543Gadc
(6) d1f6fc2435d7973a7671f8441df24980c1c24522da0fbe39c8a2df7dc9bbe2c1
(7) 6387689adfaa144f88a2e6794ba45a9c013168187c481fbc8dc533418f28d841
(8) e48fe245d67dfddf5580c0eab6eec5a29129767de4b959c9376b6b2eaa7f1cb7
(9) 3b27e53016aaa87d2200bebddf4005c243920aeebecf374a2883d400eec5d207

HD Wallet
====================
Mnemonic:      coconut hold talk build obtain talk tenant design negative
tomato choice recall
Base HD Path:  m/44'/60'/0'/0/{account_index}

Listening on localhost:8545
```

Here are some important observations to make about ganache-cli:

- Ganache is a node app that simulates the Ethereum blockchain in your PC's memory;
- It generates 10 accounts in default mode;
- The accounts are created via mnemonics and are different every time the ganache-cli is executed; and
- The RPC is launched on port 8545 of the localhost: 8545(localhost: 8545). It is through this port that Web3.Js will be accessing the Ethereum Blockchain.

Leave the right-hand side of the Terminal alone. Here we are assuming that everything will just work fine with Ethereum Blockchain. We will now turn our attention to the left-hand side of the Terminal as we test various apps on the Ethereum Blockchain. Next up, we launch Web3.Js

Launching Web3.Js

Ensure you have installed NodeJS and the required build essentials. Type the following commands the prompt if you have not installed them:

```
sudo apt-get install -y nodejs
sudo apt-get install -y build-essential
```

Use the following command to instruct the node console that you are using Web3.Js to execute your smart contracts that the Blockchain is interfacing:

```
nodejs
```

Now, point your browser to http://remix.ethereum.org and copy/paste the above code:
Here is what you should see:

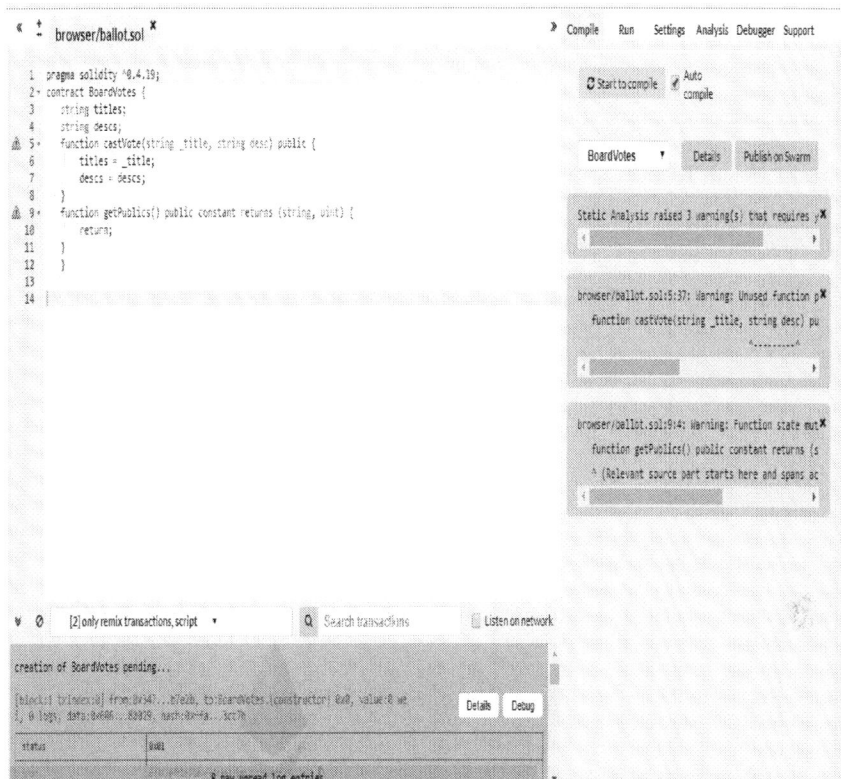

Click on the compile link to compile the smart contract if you haven't.

Now click on Run> Environment. Under Environment tab, click on Web3 Provider. Follow the onscreen instruction to activate Web3 Provider. If ganache-cli isn't running, you will not be able to use Web3 Provider.
Here is what you'll get:

The moment Web3 Provider is successfully selected, you will see the following parameters:

- Account: It is the address from which the smart contract is to be fired;
- Gas limit: The maximum value of tokens you'll be paying for the smart contracted to execute on EVM. The default value is 3000000.
- Value: The amount of Ether you have in your account. Specified in wei

As you can see from the diagram, we must start by compiling the smart contract. We will go back to the Remix IDE to help us compile the smart contract. Launch your browser and point to http://remix.ethereum.org/. Note that I'm not using https. This is because we want to change the Environment from JavaScript VM to Web3

Provider. You're likely going to encounter errors if you use https://remix.ethereum.org/

Now copy your smart contract into Remix's Editor. As usual, Remix will automatically compile it. You can check the compilation results by clicking on the Compile link>Details. Here is the output:

```
BYTECODE    ⊕

{
    "linkReferences": {},
    "object": "606060405234156100005760008062d5b60405161049d18038061049d83398101604052808051820191905050600033600080610100a1
    "opcodes": "PUSH1 0x60 PUSH1 0x40 MSTORE CALLVALUE ISZERO PUSH2 0xf JUMPI PUSH1 0x0 DUP1 REVERT JUMPDEST PUSH1 0x40 MLO
    "sourceMap": "25:839:0:-;;233:231;;;;;;;;;;;;;;;;;;;;;367:6;298:10;288:7;;20;;;;;;;;;;;;;;;336:9;16;318:1
}
```

```
ABI    ⊕

▶ 0:
▶ 1:
▶ 2:
▶ 3:
▶ 4:
▶ 5:
▶ 6:
```

```
WEB3DEPLOY    ⊕

var addresses = /* var of type address[] here */ ;
var revenuesharingContract = web3.eth.contract([{"constant":true,"inputs":[],"name":"creator","outputs":[{"name":"","type":
var revenuesharing = revenuesharingContract.new(
    addresses,
    {
        from: web3.eth.accounts[0],
        data: '0x606060405234156100005760008062d5b60403161049d38038061049d83398101604052808051820191905050600033600080610100a6',
        gas: '4700000'
    }, function (e, contract){
```

The byte-code is the binary equivalent (machine language version) of your smart contract after being compiled and the instruction set to be executed in EVM. The ABI (Application Binary Interface) is the interface that you are using to interact with the smart contract byte-code. At the bottom screen, there is Web3Deploy where the byte-code and ABI have already been bundled in preparation for deployment.

To deploy the smart contract, you need to specify a list of the target accounts. You can use the accounts beginning from the second account from eth.accounts in the ganache-cli output. Here is how to specify the accounts:

- Launch the node console window by typing the following commands:

```
nodejs
```

- Specify the accounts as follows:

```
var         addresses=[web3.eth.accounts[1],
web3.eth.accounts[2], web3.eth.accounts[3]]
```

In the above example, we are using the second account, third account and fourth account. To display these accounts, type the following command at the console:

```
addresses
```

- Now, create a class the smart contract based on the ABI. You can just copy the lines from Web3Deploy.
- Deploy the smart contract, its associated byte-code, and other necessary information. Again, you can just copy these lines from Web3Deploy.

Lab challenge

Here are lab challenges for this lesson:
1. Using the steps outlined in this chapter, perform the following actions:
    • Install NodeJS;
    • Install Web3.Js; and
    • Install ganache-cli
2. Launch your Remix Editor and copy/paste the following smart contract:

```solidity
pragma solidity ^0.4.8;

contract RevenueSharing {
    address public creator;
    mapping(uint => address) public shareholders;
    uint public numShareholders;

    event Disburse(uint _amount, uint _numShareholders);

    function RevenueSharing(address[] addresses) {
        creator = msg.sender;
        numShareholders = addresses.length;
        for (uint i=0; i< addresses.length; i++) {
            shareholders[i] = addresses[i];
        }
    }

    function shareRevenue() payable returns (bool success)  {
        uint amount = msg.value / numShareholders;
        for (uint i=0; i<numShareholders; i++) {
            if (!shareholders[i].send(amount)) revert();
        }
        Disburse(msg.value, numShareholders);
        return true;
    }

    function kill() {
        if (msg.sender == creator) selfdestruct(creator);
    }
}
```

Compile, run and deploy the above contract under Web3 Provider framework.

Summary

We have successfully programmed, compiled, deployed and executed smart contracts on the Ethereum Blockchain using Web3.Js as the development framework. Here is the summary of what we have learned so far:

- Web3.Js is the Ethereum's JavaScript API that helps users to create apps which can communicate with Ethereum nodes via JSON RPC calls. The Web3.Js libraries are available on npm (node package manager) as a node module. If you're using a browser, and its related components, you can find these libraries embedded in JavaScript.

- Ganache-cli simulates full client behavior and makes developing DApps faster, safer and easier. It incorporates all the popular RPC functions and features such as events which can be executed deterministically to fast-track the development of DApps.

- To use Web3.Js framework, execute a ganache-cli command on your Terminal and switch over to the Remix IDE. Click on the Run link, and then alter the Environment's dropdown from JavaScript VM to Web3 Provider. Follow the onscreen instructions to change the environment.

Next up, we explore smart contract events with Web3.Js.

References

1. https://medium.com/@m_mcclarty/setting-up-solidity-on-windows-10-993a1d2c615c
2. https://blockgeeks.com/guides/smart-contract-development/
3. https://ethereum.gitbooks.io/frontier-guide/content/listing_accounts.html
4. https://solidity.readthedocs.io/en/develop/
5. https://medium.com/hci-wvu/hello-world-in-solidity-3e7d3e025831

Chapter 4: Smart Contract Events with Web3.Js

Prerequisites

In this chapter, several programming assignments in Web3.Js will be introduced. No prior experience with Web3.Js is required. However, elementary programming language or prior experience with programming languages such as JavaScript or Python is essential. In addition, you'll be required to have a basic understanding of the following concepts:

- Programming in Solidity;
- HTML5 and CSS;
- Linux commands; and
- Basic Linux administration skills

Theory

Before we dive into smart contract events, let's first dissect JavaScript events.

In Web 2, JavaScript interacts with HTML through events which occur when the web user or the browser attempts to manipulate a page. Examples of JavaScript events include:

- When a web page loads;
- When a user clicks on a hyperlinked button;
- When a user presses any key on the key board;
- When a user closes a window;
- When the mouse moves over an HTML element;

- When an input field changes;
- When an HTML form is submitted; and
- When a user resizes a window.

In the example below, a function is called from the event handler to process an "onclick" event:

```
<!DOCTYPE html>
<html>
<body>
<h1   onclick="changeText(this)">Click   Here   to
change this text!</h1>
<script>
function changeText(id) {
    id.innerHTML = "Ooops! A JavaScript event has
occured";
}
</script>
</body>
</html>
```

You can use the events to run JavaScript coded responses, which will cause buttons to close the windows, messages to be shown to users, data to be confirmed, and virtually any other type of response that you can imagine of. JavaScript events are a part of the DOM (Document Object Model) Level 3 and every HTML element has a set of events which can trigger the JavaScript Code.

What about Web3.Js Events?

Events are essential in Ethereum Blockchain because, without them, they would be no meaningful communication between smart contracts and the DApp user interfaces. In conventional web development, server response is often offered in a call back to the JavaScript-enabled front-end.
Ethereum is somehow different.

Whenever nodes mine a transaction, the smart contracts often emitcertain events and write logs to the ledger for the front-end system to process. Ideally, a smart contract event will allow you to conveniently access the Ethereum Virtual Machine logging facilities and use it to call JavaScript callbacks inside the DApp's user interface.

By conveniently accessing the EVM and calling JavaScript callbacks, you'll be in a position to listen for the smart contract events. You can think of smart contracts as inheritable members of the smartcontracts in Solidity. Therefore, when eventsare called, they result in the arguments getting stored in the logs.

You can think of a transaction log as a unique data structure in Ethereum Blockchain. All transaction logs are always associated with the smart contract's address and incorporated in the Blockchain. Once included, they can stay there as long as the block is still accessible. Also, smart contracts events and transaction logs cannot be retrieved from inside the contracts (including the contracts that generated the event). Simplified Payment Verification proofs for transaction logs are often feasible when considering their modes of operations.

Therefore, in case an outside entity was to supply the smart contract with proof, it must verify that the log really does exist on the Ethereum Blockchain. Either way, you must be cognizant of the fact that block headers should be supplied because the smart contract is only able to see the last 256 block hashes.

Also, no more than 3 parameters are capable of obtaining the indexed attributes which will cause the search for each of their parameters. If you're dealing with indexed parameters, then you must ensure that they are filtered properly. In the case of arrays— including bytes and strings—you must specify the indexed arguments to allow the Keccak-256 hash be stored in an appropriate form.

In summary, there are 3 primary use cases for smart contract events and logs:

- **They return values for the front-end user interface**: Smart contract events always return value of the `sendTransaction` method as a hash of the transaction which is created;
- **They can asynchronously trigger when given data**: For instance, when the contract wants to trigger the front-end, it will emit an event. When front-end is listening for events, it will take actions and display messages; and
- **They can be used as cheaper means of storage**: Transaction logs were conceived to be a more reasonable form of storage with significantly minimal gas than the actual contract storage.

Consider the example smart contract below:

```
pragma solidity ^0.4.19;
contract Receipts {
    event DepositLogs(
        uint _value
        bytes32 indexed _ids,
        address indexed _from,
```

```
    );
    function depositFuncs(bytes32 _ids) payable {
        // All the function calls directed at that
function, including the deeply nested ones
        // will be detected by the JavaScript API
through
        // filtering in the <code data-enlighter-
language="generic"
class="EnlighterJSRAW">DepositLogs</code>  to  be
called.
        DepositLogs(msg.sender, _id, msg.value);
    }
}
```

Here is how the code will be implemented in JavaScript:

```
var abi = /* This specifies the ABI. The compiler
will automatically generate it */;
var receipts = Receipt.at("0x1234...ab67" /* the
contract's address */);
var Receipts = web3.eth.contract(abi);
var sampleEvent = receipts.Deposit();
// Now, watch to notice the changes
sampleEvent.watch(function(error, result){
    // The result will contain various info
    // that includes the arguments which has
beengiven
    // to the deposit call.
    if (!error)
        console.log(result);
});
// Or, you can start watching right away by passing
a callback as follows:
var                 sampleEvent                 =
receipts.Deposit(function(error, result) {
    if (!error)
        console.log(result);
});
```

The main aspect of the first code is the declaration and

triggering of `DepositLogs` event. In the second code, notice how the Web3.Js API listens for events and acts upon them the moment they take place. You should also note that parameters that are indexed will not be stored, meaning that you have to look for the values yourself.

Smart contract events can also asynchronously be triggered when given data. For instance, when the contract wants to trigger the front-end, it will emit an event. And if the front-end part of the DApp is listening for events, it will take actions and display messages. Such a contract will return values which are minimal use cases for the events which can be deemed as asynchronous triggers with the data.

The third use case of smart contract events is quite different from what we have learned so far. Smart contract events can offer a significantly cheaper form of storage. In the Ethereum Virtual Machine, events can be considered as logs (log opcodes). In technical terms, data can be stored in the logs as opposed to being stored in the smart contract events.

However, when we go a level higher the protocol stack, it is accurate to say that smart contracts emit or triggers events which the frontend platform can react to. In this instance, whenever an event is emitted, its corresponding logs will be written to the Blockchain.

So, what is the difference between logs and events?

Logs were conceived to be a form of storage that costs less gas compared to the contract storage. In Ethereum, logs basically costs 8 gas per each byte, whereas the smart contract storage costs 20,000 gas per every 32 bytes. Even though logs provide massive gas savings, they are not accessible from any smart contract.

Nevertheless, there are use cases for leveraging logs as cheaper form of storage, rather than triggers for the frontend. An appropriate example for logs is storing the historical data which can be rendered by the frontend part of the application. For instance, a crypto-exchange may want to show a user all deposits that he/her has performed on the exchange.

Rather than storing these deposit details in a smart contract, it would be much cheaper to store them as logs. This is possible since the crypto-exchange needs only the state of the user's balance, which will be found on the contract storage. However, the exchange doesn't need to know about the finer details of the historical deposits.

Here is a code demonstrating how a crypto-exchange can use logs as a cheaper form of storage:

```
contract Crypto_exchange {
  event Deposit(uint256 indexed _markets, address
indexed _senders, uint256 _amount, uint256 _time);
function   deposits(uint256   _amount,   uint256
_market) returns (int256) {
    // Performing deposits and updating the user's
balance, etc
    Deposit(_market, msg.sender, _amount, now);
}
```

Now, suppose you want to update a UI when a user deposits.

The code below demonstrates how to use an event (Deposit) as an asynchronous trigger with the data (_market, msg.sender, _amount, now). Here, we are assuming that the Crypto_exchange1 Contract is an instance of the Crypto_exchange:

```
var                    depositEvent           =
crypto_exchange1.Deposit({_sender: userAddress});
depositEvent.watch(function(err, result) {
  if (err) {
    console.log(err)
    return;
  }
  // append the details of result.args to the UI
})
```

Now that you have familiarized with the theory behind smart contract events let's dig in deeper to find out how you can use them in Web3.Js.

Aim

In the last chapter, we learned how to use the Ethereum ganache-cli and Web3.Js to generate a basic user interface that helped us to connect the smart contract to Ethereum Virtual Machine. In this chapter, we dive deeper to explore how Solidity events can enhance the user interface and performance of smart contracts. Here is the workflow:

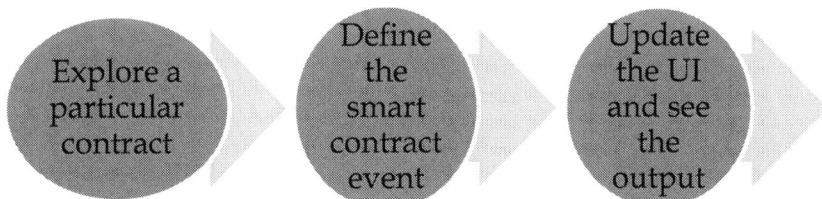

Lab Activity

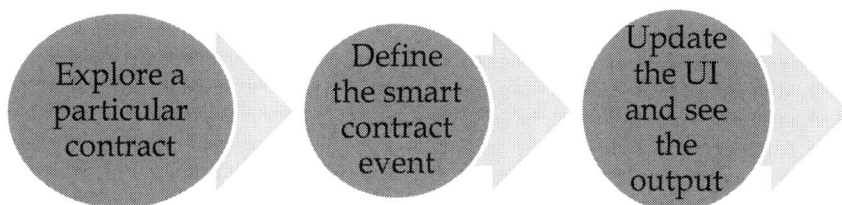

Today's lab activity will involve examining a specific smart contract in Solidity, defining the smart contract event and updating the UI.

Exploring the current smart contract

Consider a simple, smart contract below:

```
pragma solidity ^0.4.19;
contract Employees {
    string firstName;
    uint age;
    function setEmployees(string _firstName, uint
_age) public {
        firstName = _firstName;
        age = _age;
    }
    function getEmployees() view public returns
(string, uint) {
```

```
        return (firstName, age);
    }
}
```

As you can see, the first function of the code simply sets an employee's name and age. The second function gets the employee's age. As explained in the previous chapter, you can execute the code in the Web3.Js framework as follows:

- Launch the Bash Terminal and trigger ganache-cli as follows:

```
ganache-cli
```

- Now, launch your browser and point it to http://remix.ethereum.org and copy/paste the code.
- Click on Run link and select Web3 Provider under Environment tab. Here is what you'll get:

- Follow the onscreen instruction to enable Web3 Provider and click on create.

We'll now create a UI that will help us interact with the smart contract.

Launch the Terminal and open up the code editor in the node_modules folder that was created when you installed Web3.Js through npm. Navigate to the node_modules using the cd command and create an index.html in that directory as follows:

```
nano index.html
```

Here is what you'll get:

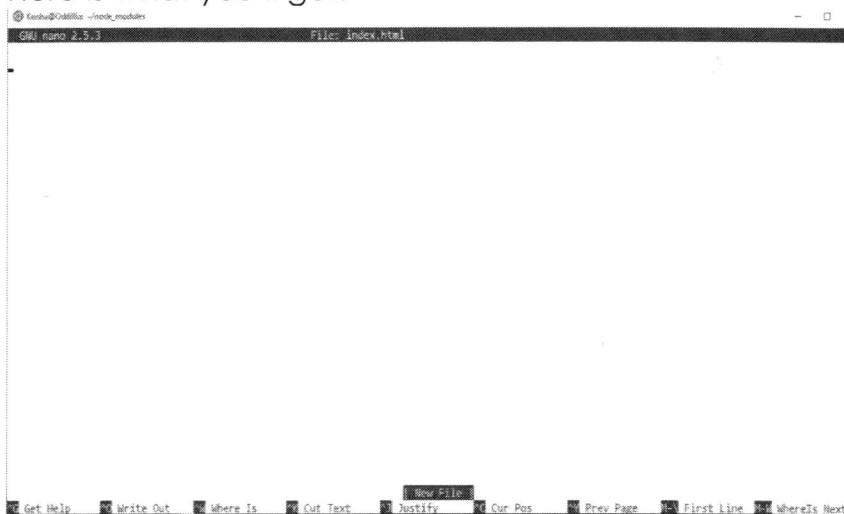

Now, we are going to create an HTML form with 2 fields: Employee Name and Employee Age. The form will retrieve Employees name and age using the getPublic () function. To get started, copy/paste the following HTML code into the index.html file:

```
<!DOCTYPE html>
<html lang="en">
```

```
<head>
    <meta charset="UTF-8">
    <meta name="viewport" content="width=device-
width, initial-scale=1.0">
    <meta            http-equiv="X-UA-Compatible"
content="ie=edge">
    <title>Welcome to Web3 Programming</title>
    <link    rel="stylesheet"    type="text/css"
href="main.css">
    <script
src="./node_modules/web3/dist/web3.min.js"></scri
pt>
</head>
<body>
    <div class="container">
        <h1>Employee Details</h1>
        <h2 id="employees"></h2>
        <label    for="name"    class="col-lg-2
control-label">Title</label>
        <input id="Employeename" type="text">
        <label    for="name"    class="col-lg-2
control-label">Descriptionlabel>
        <input id="age" type="text">
        <button id="button">SetEmployees</button>
    </div>
    <script src="https://code.jquery.com/jquery-
3.2.1.slim.min.js"></script>
    <script>
        // Our future code will go here…
    </script>
</body>
</html>
```

Press Ctrl+O to save the contents in index.html.

If you want to reference the `main.css` file in the node_modules folder, just copy/paste in the following code:

```
body {
    background-color:#F1F2Fb;
```

```
    padding: 3em;
    font-family:  'Raleway','Source  Sans  Pro',
'Times New Roman';
}
.container {
    width: 60%;
    margin: 1 auto;
}
label {
    display:block;
    margin-bottom:11px;
}
input {
    padding:12px;
    width: 50%;
    margin-bottom: 2em;
}
button {
    margin: 2em 0;
    padding: 2em 4em;
    display:block;
}
#employee {
    padding:2em;
    background-color:#2200ff;
    margin: 1em 0;
}
```

Now save the file.

The next step involves coding the Web3.Js for connecting and interacting with the smart contract.

Go back to the index.html file using the command below:

```
nano index.html
```

At the bottom of the file, you'll find an empty <script>

tag. It is in the <script> tags that we'll write the necessary code to interface with our smart contract. Therefore, proceed to copy/paste the following code:

```
<script>
        if (typeof web3 !== 'undefined') {
            web3                =            new
Web3(web3.currentProvider);
        } else {
            // set the provider you want from
Web3.providers such as
            //JavaScript VM or Injected Web
            web3      =      new      Web3      (new
Web3.providers.HttpProvider
("http://localhost:8545"));
        }
    </script>
```

Here is the complete code for index.html file:

```
<!DOCTYPE html>
<html lang="en">
<head>
    <meta charset="UTF-8">
    <meta name="viewport" content="width=device-
width, initial-scale=1.0">
    <meta            http-equiv="X-UA-Compatible"
content="ie=edge">
    <title>Welcome to Web3 Programming</title>
    <link    rel="stylesheet"    type="text/css"
href="main.css">
    <script
src="./node_modules/web3/dist/web3.min.js"></scri
pt>
</head>
<body>
    <div class="container">
        <h1>Employee Details</h1>
        <h2 id="employees"></h2>
```

```
        <label      for="name"      class="col-lg-2
control-label">Title</label>
        <input id="Employeename" type="text">
        <label      for="name"      class="col-lg-2
control-label">Descriptionlabel>
        <input id="age" type="text">
        <button id="button">SetEmployees</button>
    </div>
    <script  src="https://code.jquery.com/jquery-
3.2.1.slim.min.js"></script>
    <script>

        if (typeof web3 !== 'undefined') {
            web3          =          new
Web3(web3.currentProvider);
        } else {
            // set to a provider of your choice
            web3    =    new    Web3(new
Web3.providers.HttpProvider("http://localhost:854
5"));
        }

        web3.eth.defaultAccount          =
web3.eth.accounts[0];
        var        employeesContract        =
web3.eth.contract('PASTE the ABI HERE!');

    </script>
</body>
</html>
```

Next, we find out how you can specify an event to facilitate the communication to Ethereum's virtual machine.

Defining the Smart Contract Event

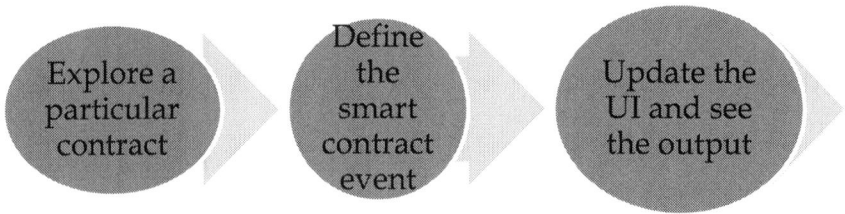

As mentioned earlier, an event will allow you to access the Ethereum Virtual Machine logging facilities conveniently. You can use the event to call JavaScript callbacks inside the DApp's user interface. In this example, we want to specify an event that takes place when the employee's name is set using the function `setEmployees (string _firstName, uint _age)`

Here is how you can create an event that is triggered when the employee's name is set:

```
event    Employees(string    employee_name,uint
employee_age
    );
```

As you can see in the above code, we are passing in two types that represent the `employee_name` and `employee_age`. If the event is successfully returned to our UI, we can comfortably access these values. To use the event (event Employees), you must call the event and pass in the submitted employee name and age within the `setEmployees ()` function as follows:

```
function  setEmployees(string   _firstName,   uint
_age) public {
      firstName = _firstName;
      age = _age;
      Employees(_firstName, _age);
   }
```

Notice that we are using the same function only that this time we are adding the event function (`Employees(_firstName, _age);`).

So, what is the effect of adding the event function? When the `setEmployees` () is initiated by a user who clicks the Set Employees button in the user interface, an event is automatically generated. As a result, you can listen to it via the conventional JavaScript and figure out when to hide the loading graphic.

It's now time to update the user interface.

Updating the UI

From the previous discussion, here is the current script for interfacing the smart contract:

```
<script>
        if (typeof web3 !== 'undefined') {
            web3        =        new        Web3
(web3.currentProvider);
        } else {
            // set to a provider of your choice
            web3        =        new        Web3(new
Web3.providers.HttpProvider("http://localhost:854
5"));
        }
        web3.eth.defaultAccount        =
web3.eth.accounts [0];
        var        employeesContract        =
web3.eth.contract('Copy/Paste the ABI code here');
    </script>
```

Now, add the following code under the <script> and </script> tags:

```
<script>
        if (typeof web3 !== 'undefined') {
            web3        =        new        Web3
(web3.currentProvider);
        } else {
            // set to a provider of your choice
            web3       =       new       Web3(new
Web3.providers.HttpProvider("http://localhost:854
5"));
        }
        web3.eth.defaultAccount               =
web3.eth.accounts [0];
        var           employeesContract           =
web3.eth.contract('Copy/Paste the ABI code here');
function  setEmployees(string  _firstName,  uint
_age) public {
        firstName = _firstName;
        age = _age;
        Employees(_firstName, _age);
    }
}
</script>
```

It is now time to compile and run the code.
As always start the ganache-cli as follows:

```
ganache-cli
```

Now, copy/paste the entire code into the index.html file.
Here is the entire code:

```
<!DOCTYPE html>
<html lang="en">
<head>
    <meta charset="UTF-8">
    <meta  name="viewport"  content="width=device-
width, initial-scale=1.0">
```

```html
    <meta            http-equiv="X-UA-Compatible"
content="ie=edge">
    <title>Welcome to Web3 Programming</title>
    <link      rel="stylesheet"      type="text/css"
href="main.css">
    <script
src="./node_modules/web3/dist/web3.min.js"></scri
pt>
</head>
<body>
    <div class="container">
        <h1>Employee Details</h1>
        <h2 id="employees"></h2>
        <label      for="name"      class="col-lg-2
control-label">Title</label>
        <input id="Employeename" type="text">
        <label      for="name"      class="col-lg-2
control-label">Descriptionlabel>
        <input id="age" type="text">
        <button id="button">SetEmployees</button>
    </div>
    <script  src="https://code.jquery.com/jquery-
3.2.1.slim.min.js"></script>
    <script>
        if (typeof web3 !== 'undefined') {
            web3        =        new        Web3
(web3.currentProvider);
        } else {
            // set to a provider of your choice
            web3        =        new        Web3(new
Web3.providers.HttpProvider("http://localhost:854
5"));
        }
        web3.eth.defaultAccount                 =
web3.eth.accounts [0];
        var           employeesContract           =
web3.eth.contract('Copy/Paste the ABI code here');
function    setEmployees(string    _firstName,    uint
_age) public {
        firstName = _firstName;
        age = _age;
```

```
        Employees(_firstName, _age);
    }
}
</script>
</body>
</html>
```

Lab challenge

Use the information provided in the form below to create a smart contract event that can help to interface with EVM.

First name:

Last name:

Submit

Summary

This chapter has explored how you can you can apply smart contract events to facilitate communication between a DApp and the EVM. In a nutshell, events facilitate meaningful communication between smart contracts and the DApp UIs. Whenever nodes mine a transaction, the smart contracts emit certain events and write logs to the Blockchain for the front-end system to process.

References

1. https://media.consensys.net/technical-introduction-to-events-and-logs-in-ethereum-a074d65dd61e
2. http://solidity.readthedocs.io/en/v0.4.21/contracts.html
3. https://github.com/ethchange/smart-exchange/blob/master/lib/exchange_transactions.js
4. https://github.com/ethchange/smart-exchange/blob/master/lib/contracts/SmartExchange.sol
5. https://coursetro.com/posts/code/100/Solidity-Events-Tutorial---Using-Web3.js-to-Listen-for-Smart-Contract-Events

Chapter 5: Functions, Mappings, and Structs

Prerequisites

Before embarking on this chapter, you should be familiar with the following:
- HTML5 and CSS;
- JavaScript functions;
- Remix and Solidity (Covered in chapter 1 and 2); and
- Events in Solidity (Covered in chapter 3)

Theory

Before we delve deeper to explore these concepts, a deeper understanding of how each is used in programming is important.

#1: Functions

No Blockchain developer wants to keep repeating the same task—it becomes tedious and boring. When you specify a function, you'll be defining a package of code that you can use over and over to perform the same job. All you have to do is inform EVM to perform the specific task by invoking the name of the function that you have defined

The EVM will faithfully run each instruction in the function each time you ask it to do so. When you use functions, the code that wants services from the function will be called the caller. The caller calls upon the function to perform specific tasks for it. Much of the data that you'll see about functions will refer to the caller.

The caller must provide enough data to the function for the function to return information to the caller. If Web3.Js didn't have functions, you would have to keep re-inventing the same code. The concept of functions in Web3.Js has evolved over time making Web3 to one of the most flexible languages in existence.

Functions and code reusability are a necessary part of program development because:
- They reduce the development time;
- They minimize errors during coding;
- They maximize application reliability;
- They allow entire groups to use a code from one programmer;
- They make the code easier to understand; and
- They enhance the efficiency of the code

#2: Mappings

In most languages, mappings are the name given to a higher-order function that applies a specific function to each element of a list and returns the list in the same order. You could think of mapping as an apply-to-all if you used in a functional form. But the concept of mappings isn't just limited to lists.

It also applies to sequential containers, tree-like containers and even abstract containers like promises and futures.

Consider the example below:

Suppose you have a list of integers [10, 20, 30, 40, 50] and would like to compute the square of each list integer. To do this, you must first define a function to help you square a single number such as:

```
square n = n * n
```

Afterward, you may call the map to display the results as follows:

```
map square[[10, 20, 30, 40, 50]
```

The above code will yield [100, 400, 900, 1600, 2500] as an output. This means that the map has combed through the complete list and applied the function square to each integer in the list. In most languages—Web3.Js included—a map is often provided as part of the language's standard library.

Maps are similar to objects in the sense that both of them lets you set keys to values, access those values, delete them, and detect whether something has been stored at a particular key. Because of this, maps have always been used as objects. However, there are significant differences that exist between maps and objects:
- While the keys of an object will always be strings and symbols, a map can contain any value including the objects, functions and any primitive data types;

- You must use manual means to get the number of properties of an object. For maps, you can use the size property; and
- Maps can be iterated while objects require the keys to be obtained in some fashion before iteration.

#3: Structs

Sometimes you may want to share objects by reference to enhance performance and improve the efficiency of your app. If you don't want the sharing of objects to be mutable, you may consider many objects sharing a common entity without bothering if one of them has inadvertently changed the common entity.

Various languages provide different ways of getting around the problem of mutability. In JavaScript, you can specify the variable as follows:

```
var rentValue = {};
Object.defineProperty(rentValue, 'dollars', {
  enumerable: true,
  writable: false,
  value: 600
});
Object.defineProperty(rentValue, 'cents', {
  enumerable: true,
  writable: false,
  value: 0
});
```

In the above code, `rentValue.dollars` will generate 600. However, if you want to change the value, you'll be forced to change the line as follows:

```
rentValue.dollars=800;
```

If you enforce a function that is strict such as the one below, you'll obtain a type error since the object cannot assign read-only property (dollars)

```
!function () {
  "use strict"
  rentValue.dollars = 600;
}();
```

In the above instance, you can think of the `Object.defineProperty` as a general-purpose function for offering fine-grained control over any properties that you'll define for the object. Whenever you make a property enumerable, it will show up when you list iterate the object's items or its properties.

And when you make it writable, any assignments to the property will alter its value. On the other hand, if the property is not writable, then any assignments to it are ignored. If you want to specify multiple properties, you can also write:

```
var rentValue = {};
Object.defineProperties(rentValue, {
  dollars: {
    enumerable: true,
    writable: false,
    value: 600
  },
  cents: {
    enumerable: true,
    writable: false,
    value: 0
  }
});
```

Here, `rentValue.dollars` will produce 600.
You can make the properties immutable, but this will not prevent you from adding properties to the object.

```
rentValue.feedbackComments = []
rentValue.feedbackComments.push("The  rent  amount
is too high.")
rentValue
```

In the above example, immutable properties will make the object to be closed for any modification. However, this doesn't mean that you have closed it completely for any future extension. To achieve complete immutability, you can use the code below:

```
Object.preventExtensions(rentValue);
function addCurrency(amount,  currency) {
   "use strict";
   amount.currency = currency;
   return currency;
}
```

The above code is completely immutable because any alterations will generate an error. So, how can structs help?
Majority of languages have a formal data structure which has one or more named properties which are always open for modification but closed for extension. Here is such an example:

```
function Structs (template) {
   if (Struct.prototype.isPrototypeOf(this)) {
     var structs = this;
     Object.keys(template).forEach(function  (key)
{
        Object.defineProperty(structs, key, {
```

97

```
        enumerable: true,
        writable: true,
        value: template[key]
      });
    });
    return Object.preventExtensions(structs);
  }
  else return new Structs(template);
}
var rentValue2 = Structs({dollars: 600, cents:
0});
addCurrency(rentValue2, "ISK");
```

The above code demonstrates an immutable code that is opened for modification but closed for any future extension. If you want an ImmutableStruct, consider the code below:

```
function ImmutableStructs (template) {

  if
(ImmutableStructs.prototype.isPrototypeOf(this))
{
    var immutableObjects = this;
    Object.keys(template).forEach(function  (key)
{
      Object.defineProperty(immutableObjects,
key, {
        enumerable: true,
        writable: false,
        value: template[key]
      });
    });
    return
Object.preventExtensions(immutableObjects);
  }
  else return new ImmutableStructs(template);
}
ImmutableStructs.prototype = new Structs({});
function copyValue(to, from) {
```

```
  "use strict"
  to.dollars = from.dollars;
  to.cents   = from.cents;
  return to;
}
var  immutableRent  =  ImmutableStructs({dollars:
2000, cents: 0});
copyValue(immutableRent, rentValue);
```

As you can see, structs can come in handy whenever you want to prevent inadvertent bugs and to communicate which objects should be used in the app explicitly.

Now that you have mastered what functions, mappings and structs are, let's dive in to explore how you can use them in Web3.Js.

Aim

In the previous chapter, we learned how to use smart contract events in Solidity. Specifically, we learned how to generate events, update the UI and deploy the smart contract under Web3 Provider environment. This chapter dives deeper to provide you a practical overview of functions, mappings, and structs.

Specifically, we will create a modifier that allows the smart contract to execute up to up a certain limit using the setEmployees () that we had already defined in the previous chapter. Ultimately, we will use mappings and structs to restructure the smart contract so that it incorporates many employees and their related data.

Are you ready?

Lab Task 1

Today's lab task is simple: creating a smart contract, creating a modifier, using the modifier and how to handle the modifier. Here's the workflow:

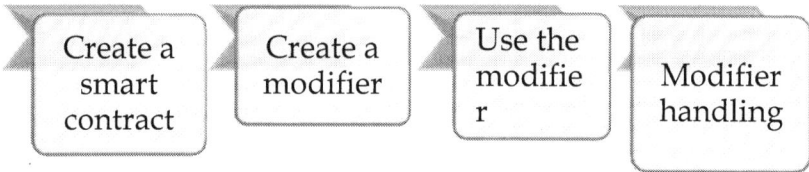

Create a smart contract → Create a modifier → Use the modifier → Modifier handling

#1: Smart contract

In the previous examples, we've been using the Employees contract to demonstrate various concepts. In this chapter, we shall use the same contract. In case you've forgotten the contract, consider this:

```solidity
pragma solidity ^0.4.19;
contract Employees {
    string firstName;
    uint age;
    event Employees(
        string employee_name,
        uint age
    );
    function setEmployees(string _firstName, uint _age) public {
        firstName = _firstName;
        age = _age;
        Employees(_firstName, _age);
    }
    function getEmployees() view public returns (string, uint) {
        return (firstName, age);
```

```
    }
}
```

In case you are stumbling upon this chapter for the first time, you may want to test whether the code compiles on Remix IDE or not. Here is a quick process of compiling and running the code in Remix IDE under Web3 Provider:

- Launch the Bash Terminal and trigger ganache-cli as follows:

```
ganache-cli
```

- Now, launch your browser and point it to http://remix.ethereum.org and copy/paste the code.
- Click on Run link and select Web3 Provider under Environment tab.
- Follow the onscreen instruction to enable Web3 Provider and click on create.

Next, we create a modifier for the smart contract

#2: Smart contract modifier

There are various reasons that compel you to use function modifiers. Here are some of the reasons:
- To reduce the development time;
- To minimize errors during coding;
- To maximize DApp's reliability;
- To allow entire groups to use the code from a single Blockchain developer;
- To add functionality to the smart contract;
- To make the code easier to understand; and
- To enhance the efficiency of the code

In this example, we will use the function modifier to add functionality to the smart contract. Specifically, we will use the function modifier to set the employee name and age via the setEmployees () method. To achieve this, you must characterize another variable as an address.

Consider the code below:

```
contract Employees {
    string firstName;
    uint age;
    address owner;//Add this line
```

Notice that we have used the same code but added another line: address owner.

Next, we need to call a constructor with an end goal to help set the proprietor variable to the address that has just made the contract. Here, the constructor function will be called once, and it will define the point at which the smart contract was first made. Here is the code to do this:

```
contract Employees{
        string firstName;
    uint age;
    address owner;
        function Employees() public {      // Add
this constructor
        owner = msg.sender;
    }
```

Now that you know the proprietor contains the maker's contract address, you can create a modifier underneath the constructor as follows:

```
modifier onlyOwner {
    require(msg.sender == owner);
    _;
}
```

As you can see, creating a modifier requires you first to express its name. In our case, the name of the modifier is `onlyOwner`. This modifier can now be utilized in various instances depending on your necessities.

So, how can you use the modifier? The next section describes how you can apply a modifier.

#3: Using the modifier

Once you define your modifier, you can utilize it in any function so long as it makes sense. In our example, we will be using it in the Employees contract. Therefore, we'll include it in the setEmployees () function as follows:

```
setEmployees() function:
    function setEmployees(string _firstName, uint
_age) onlyOwner public {
        firstName = _firstName;
        age = _age;
        Employees(_firstName, _age);
    }
```

Notice that `onlyOwner` is written immediately after the defining the `setEmployees` () function. You can now compile and run the code by following the steps below:

- Launch the Bash Terminal and trigger ganache-cli as follows:

```
ganache-cli
```

- Now, launch your browser and point it to http://remix.ethereum.org and copy/paste the code.
- Click on Run link and select Web3 Provider under Environment tab.
- Follow the onscreen instruction to enable Web3 Provider and click on create.

Lab Task 2

In this lab session, we'll create a mapping and structs and demonstrate how to use them. Here is the workflow:

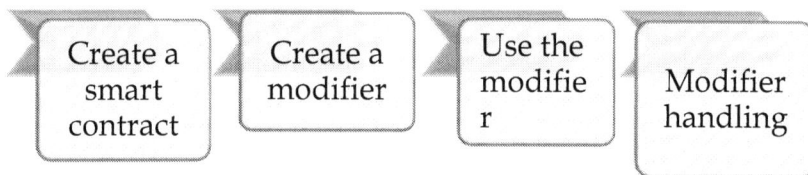

| Create a smart contract | Create a modifier | Use the modifier | Modifier handling |

#1: Create a Structs

In Solidity, a struct is just a custom type that any Blockchain developer can define. To define a struct, you must specify its name and the associated properties. Here is a quick way to define a struct:

- Launch your browser and point to http://remix.ethereum.org/ to start the Remix IDE Editor
- Start a new file in the Remix IDE Editor. You can give it any name.
- Copy/paste the following code:

```
pragma solidity ^0.4.19;
```

104

```
contract Jobs {
    struct Employees {
        uint age;
        string firstName;
        string lastName;
    }
}
```

You can now compile and run the code by following the steps below:

- Launch the Bash Terminal and trigger ganache-cli as follows:

```
ganache-cli
```

- Now, launch your browser and point it to http://remix.ethereum.org and copy/paste the code.
- Click on Run link and select Web3 Provider under Environment tab.
- Follow the onscreen instruction to enable Web3 Provider and click on create.

#2: Create a mapping

In Solidity, a mapping is simply a hash table that comprises the key. Here is a quick way to create a mapping:

- Launch your browser and point to http://remix.ethereum.org/ to start the Remix IDE Editor
- Start a new file in the Remix IDE Editor. You can give it any name.
- Copy/paste the following code:

```
contract Jobs {
```

```
struct Employees {
    uint age;
    string firstName;
    string lastName;
}
mapping (address => Employees) employees;
address[] public employeesAccts;
}
```

You can now compile and run the code by following the steps below:

- Launch the Bash Terminal and trigger ganache-cli as follows:

```
ganache-cli
```

- Now, launch your browser and point it to http://remix.ethereum.org and copy/paste the code.
- Click on Run link and select Web3 Provider under Environment tab.
- Follow the onscreen instruction to enable Web3 Provider and click on create.

In the above example, we've created a mapping that acknowledges the key sort where it can write and compose just as the Struct is used. The mapping data structure will allow you to look into a specific employee with his/her Ethereum address and retrieve the first name, last name, and age.

#3: Map additions

Consider the code below:

```
function setEmployees(address _address, uint
_age, string _firstName, string _lastName) public
{
```

```
    var employees = employees[_address];
    employees.age = _age;
    employees.firstName = _firstName;
    employee.lastName = _lName;
            employeesAccts.push(_address) -1;
}
```

You can now compile and run the code by following the steps below:

- Launch the Bash Terminal and trigger ganache-cli as follows:

```
ganache-cli
```

- Now, launch your browser and point it to http://remix.ethereum.org and copy/paste the code.
- Click on Run link and select Web3 Provider under Environment tab.
- Follow the onscreen instruction to enable Web3 Provider and click on create.

In the above code, we have passed an address, age, first name and last name of the function. Next, the variable employees have been made restricted to the employees mapping as a _address in the key. Once you've defined the mappings, you can now set the age, first name and last name as espoused in the code. At the end of the code, we push the new employee to the variety of addresses on employeesAccts.

Lab challenge

Use the Remix IDE Editor and Web3.Js to create, compile and run:

- 2 modifiers;
- 2 mappings; and
- 2 structs

Summary

This chapter has explored how you can you can use functions, structs, and mappings to enhance your code-ability skills in Solidity and Web3.Js. Here are the key takeaways from the chapter:

- Functions define a package of code that you can use over and over to perform the same job. By invoking the name of the function that you have already defined, you'll be directing the EVM to perform the specific functional tasks.
- Maps are similar to objects in the sense that both of them allows the developer to set keys to values, access those values, delete them, and detect whether something has been stored.
- A struct is a formal data structure which has one or more named properties which are always open for modification but closed for extension.

By now, you should be in a position to create and use functions, structs, and mappings in Solidity and Web3.Js. The next chapter examines inheritance and deployment in Solidity.

References

1. http://raganwald.com/2014/06/15/immutable-structs.html

2. https://developer.mozilla.org/en-US/docs/Web/JavaScript/Reference/Global_Objects/Map
3. https://www.w3schools.com/jsref/jsref_map.asp
4. https://en.wikipedia.org/wiki/Struct_(C_programming_language)
5. https://solidity.readthedocs.io/en/develop/

Chapter 6: Inheritance and Deployment

Prerequisites

This chapter introduces object orientation concepts in Web3.Js and Solidity. Emphasis is placed on inheritance and deployment of DApps in Web3.Js and Solidity. As such, the chapter will require a solid understanding and mastery of the following concepts:

- Functional or procedural programming;
- Object-oriented programming concepts such as inheritance, polymorphism, abstraction and encapsulation; and
- Knowledge of Solidity (Covered in chapter 1 and 2).

Theory

This section explores the inheritance and deployment concepts in Web3.Js and Solidity.

#1: Inheritance

In an object-oriented system, inheritance allows new objects to be created based on the characteristics of existing objects. A class that forms the basis for inheritance is called a superclass or base class while the class which inherits from the base class is called a derived class or subclass.

During inheritance, a child inherits all the visible properties and methods from the base class while adding extra characteristics and functions of its own. You can think of base and derived classes regarding relationships. For example, an orange fruit is an instance of a citrus fruit, which is just a fruit.

Because orange is a fruit, it is appropriate to write an Orange class as a subclass of the Fruit class. In contrast, a kitchen has a sink. Therefore, it would not make sense to impute that a kitchen is a sink or that a sink is a kitchen. This kind of relationship is called a "has-a" relationship and defines composition rather than inheritance.

The diagram below summarizes inheritance for the Orange Class:

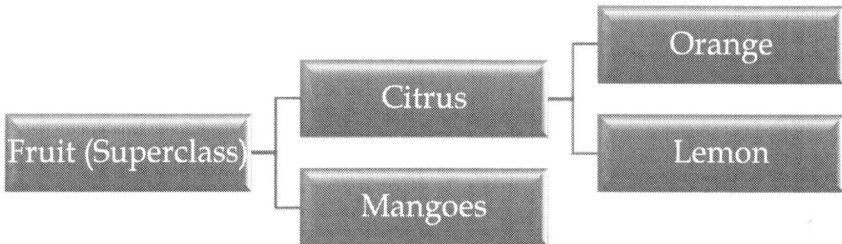

```
                                        ┌─────────────┐
                                        │   Orange    │
                          ┌──────────┐  │             │
                          │  Citrus  │──┤
┌──────────────────┐      │          │  │             │
│ Fruit (Superclass)│─────┤          │  └─────────────┘
│                  │      └──────────┘  ┌─────────────┐
│                  │      ┌──────────┐  │   Lemon     │
└──────────────────┘      │ Mangoes  │
                          │          │
                          └──────────┘
```

So, how is inheritance handled in Solidity?

Solidity supports multiple inheritances by copying the smart contract code including polymorphism. Since all the function calls are virtual, it is the most derived function that will be called unless you explicitly specifies otherwise. Even if the smart contract inherits from multiple super contracts, only a single contract will be created on the Blockchain.

The code from the base contracts will always be copied onto the final contract.

Consider the following Solidity code:

```
contract owned {
    function owned() { owner = msg.sender; }
    address owner;
}
```

To inherit from the owned contract, we will use the keyword "is' to derive another contract. In this case, the derived contracts access all the non-private members including the state variables and internal functions of owned contract.

Here is an example:

```
contract mortal is owned {
    function kills() {
        if       (msg.sender       ==       owner)
selfdestruct(owner);
    }
}
```

Abstract contracts are only provided to allow the interface to be known to the EVM. If a smart contract doesn't implement all the internal functions, it can only be applied as an interface.

Consider the code below:

```
contract Configuration {
```

```
    function lookups(uint id) returns (address
adr);
}
contract NameReg {
    function registers(bytes32 name);
    function unregisters();
}
```

Multiple inheritances are also possible in Solidity. In the above example, "owned" is a base class of the "mortal" class, yet there is only a single instance of "owned" in the code.

Here is a code that supports multiple inheritances:

```
contract named is owned, mortal {
    function named(bytes32 name) {
        Configuration         config        =
Configuration(0xd5f9d8d94886e70b06e474c3fb14fd43e
2f23970);

NameReg(config.lookups(1)).registers(name);
    }
```

Just like OOP languages, functions can be overridden. In this case, both local and the message-based function calls override them into the accounts as follows:

```
    function kills() {
        if (msg.sender == owner) {
            Configuration         config        =
Configuration(0xd5f9d8d94886e70b06e474c3fb14fd43e
2f23970);

NameReg(config.lookups(1)).unregisters();
            // You can still call a specific
            // overridden function as follows:
            mortal.kills();
```

```
        }
    }
}
```

If a constructor takes a parameter, it needs to be given the header (or modifier-invocation-style at the constructor of the child contract as shown below:

```
contract     PriceFeeds     is     owned,     mortal,
named("GoldFeed") {
   function updatesInfo(uint newInfo) {
      if (msg.sender == owner) info = newInfo;
   }
   function  get()  constant  returns(uint  r)  {
return info; }
   uint info;
}
```

Notice that we call `mortal.kills()` to forward the destruction request. However, this can be problematic as illustrated below:

```
contract mortal is owned {
    function kills() {
        if         (msg.sender        ==        owner)
selfdestruct(owner);
    }
}
contract Parent1 is mortal {
    function  kills()  {  /*  do  cleanup  1  */
mortal.kills(); }
}
contract Parent2 is mortal {
    function  kills()  {  /*  do  cleanup  2  */
mortal.kills(); }
}
contract Final is Parent1, Parent2 {
}
```

In the above example, a call to `Final.kills()` will call `Parent2.kills` as the most derived override. However, this function will bypass `Parent1.kills` because it doesn't even know about `Parent1`. The way around this problem is to use super as follows:

```
contract mortal is owned {
    function kills() {
        if        (msg.sender     ==      owner)
selfdestruct(owner);
    }
}
contract Parent1 is mortal {
    function  kills()  {  /*  do  cleanup  1  */
super.kills(); }
}
contract Base2 is mortal {
    function  kill()  {  /*  do  cleanup  2  */
super.kills(); }
}
contract Final is Parent2, Parent1 {
}
```

If `Parent1` calls a function of super, it doesn't just call this function on one of its parent contracts. Instead, it calls this function on the next parent contract in the final inheritance graph, so it will call `Parent2.kill`. Note that the final inheritance sequence is beginning with the most subclass contract: `Final,  Parent1,  Parent2, mortal, and owned`.

Next, we examine the process of deploying smart contracts.

#2: Deployment

In chapter 1, we learned how Solidity smart contracts

are compiled. In a sense, the EVM does not translate the Solidity code as it is. It has to be compiled down to the EVM byte-code that provides extra information about the smart contract. There are 2 properties that you'll need to deploy your smart contract:

- **ABI (Application Binary Interface):** It is the standard protocol of interacting with smart contracts on the Ethereum Blockchain, both from outside the Blockchain and for the contract-to-contract interactions.
- **Byte-code:** It is the code that the EVM will execute.

Here is a simplified workflow of smart contract compilation and deployment:

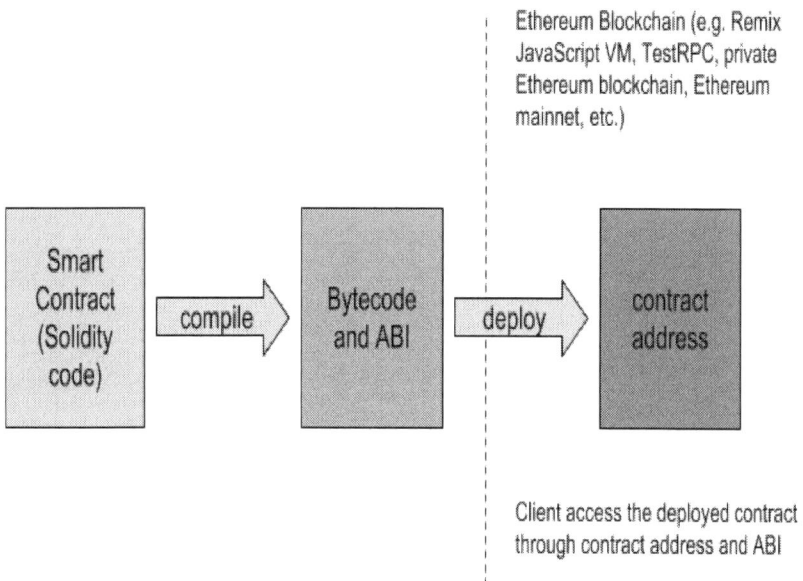

Ethereum Blockchain (e.g. Remix JavaScript VM, TestRPC, private Ethereum blockchain, Ethereum mainnet, etc.)

Smart Contract (Solidity code) → compile → Bytecode and ABI → deploy → contract address

Client access the deployed contract through contract address and ABI

Source: Blockgeeks.com

After mastering inheritance and deployment concepts, what next?

Well, it's time to get hands-on practical to see how they apply to smart contracts.

Aim

As mentioned, inheritance can help you characterize a smart parent contract, from which various contracts can be derived. In a sense, inheritance allows you to reuse the parent contracts in the future contracts without rewriting the same code. So far, we've only been working on a single smart contract.

In this section, we demonstrate how you can apply inheritance in smart contracts. We'll also learn how to deploy the smart contract. Here is the workflow:

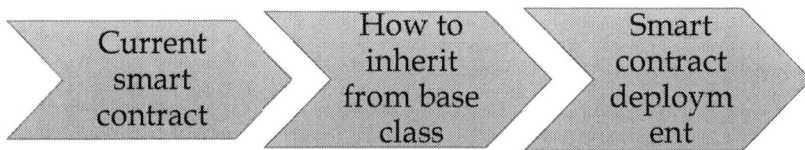

Current smart contract → How to inherit from base class → Smart contract deployment

#1: Current smart contract

Consider the following smart contract:

```
pragma solidity ^0.4.19;
contract Courses {
    struct Instructor {
        uint age;
        string firstName;
        string lastName;
    }
    mapping (address => Instructor) instructors;
    address[] public instructorAccounts;
```

117

```
    function setInstructor(address _address, uint
_age, string _firstName, string _lastName) public
{
        var instructor = instructors[_address];
        instructor.age = _age;
        instructor.fName = _firstName;
        instructor.lName = _lastName;
        instructorAccounts.push(_address) -1;
    }
    function    getInstructors()    view    public
returns(address[]) {
        return instructorAccounts;
    }
    function getInstructor(address _address) view
public returns (uint, string, string) {
        return          (instructors[_address].age,
instructors[_address].firstName,
instructors[_address].lastName);
    }
    function    countInstructors()    view    public
returns (uint) {
        return instructorAccounts.length;
    }
}
```

If you've just stumbled on this chapter for the first time, just copy/paste this code into the Remix Editor, run the ganache-cli and compile the code under Web3 Provider environment using the steps below:

- Launch the Bash Terminal and trigger ganache-cli as follows:

```
ganache-cli
```

- Now, launch your browser and point it to http://remix.ethereum.org and copy/paste the code.

118

- Click on Run link and select Web3 Provider under Environment tab.
- Follow the onscreen instruction to enable Web3 Provider and click on create.

If you keenly examine the code, you'll realize that it only has one contract (Courses). What if you wanted to create many instances of the Courses contracts? You'll need to apply inheritance as explained in the preceding section.

#2: How to inherit in Solidity

The first thing that you should come to mind whenever you want to inherit is to define the owner address and the modifier that provides the owner the capability to access particular functions. Here is how you can define the base class from our smart contract:

```
pragma solidity ^0.4.19;
contract Owned {
    address owner;
    function Owned() public {
        owner = msg.sender;
    }
    modifier onlyOwner {
        require(msg.sender == owner);
        _;
    }
}
contract Courses is Owned {
// The other code is removed for brevity
```

In the above code, we are simply setting the owner address to the creator of the smart contract, and a given modifier. Notice how we have added "is Owned" onto the smart contract. Essentially, the contract named

Courses is now owned by the creator defined earlier.

We can make sure that this works by adding the "onlyOwner" modifier in the setInstructor method in the inherited smart contract as follows:

```
// The other code has been removed for brevity
function setInstructor(address _address, uint
_age, bytes16 _firstName, bytes16 _lastName)
onlyOwner public {
// The other code has been removed for brevity
```

If you implement this contract and attempt to set an instructor as you've been doing in this previous chapters, it will only work if you have set it with the address that was used for deploying the contract.

This will work because the Courses contracted is inheriting from the Owned contract. You can even pass in the parameters from inherited contracts. For instance, our smart contract has 2 strings: first name and last name. Strings are less efficient on EVM. If possible, you should use bytes by modifying the contract so that each reference of a first and last name is bytes16 instead.

Here is the full smart contract after the necessary inheritance changes have been made:

```
pragma solidity ^0.4.19;
contract Owned {
    address owner;
    function Owned() public {
        owner = msg.sender;
    }
  modifier onlyOwner {
      require(msg.sender == owner);
```

```
        _;
    }
}
contract Courses is Owned {
    struct Instructor {
        uint age;
        bytes16 firstName;
        bytes16 lastName;
    }
    mapping (address => Instructor) instructors;
    address[] public instructorAccounts;
    event instructorInfo(
        bytes16 firstName,
        bytes16 lastName,
        uint age
    );
    function setInstructor(address _address, uint
_age, bytes16 _firstName, bytes16 _lastName)
onlyOwner public {
        var instructor = instructors[_address];
        instructor.age = _age;
        instructor.firstName = _firstName;
        instructor.lastName = _lastName;
        instructorAccounts.push(_address) -1;
        instructorInfo(_firstName,    _lastName,
_age);
    }
    function   getInstructors()   view   public
returns(address[]) {
        return instructorAccounts;
    }
    function getInstructor(address _address) view
public returns (uint, bytes16, bytes16) {
        return       (instructors[_address].age,
instructors[_address].firstName,
instructors[_address].lastName);
    }
    function   countInstructors()   view   public
returns (uint) {
        return instructorAccounts.length;
    }
```

```
}
```

To run the code in Remix Editor, just copy/paste it and activate Web3 Provider by clicking Run>Environment. Under Environment, select Web3 Provider and follow the onscreen instructions to activate Web3 Provider. When you click on create button, here is what you should see:

Compile	Run	Settings	Analysis	Debugger	Support

Environment   Web3 ProviderCustom (1523339733265) ▼ **i**

Account   0x0da...a7202 (99.9999999999994373{ ▼ 📋 ‹

Gas limit   3000000

Value   0 | **wei** ▼

Courses ▼

| | Create |
| Load contract from Address | At Address |

0 pending transactions   💾 ▶ 🗑

✖

▾   Courses at 0x312...597fd (blockchain)   📋

setInstructor	address _address, uint256
countInstructors	
getInstructor	address _address
getInstructors	
instructorAccounts	uint256

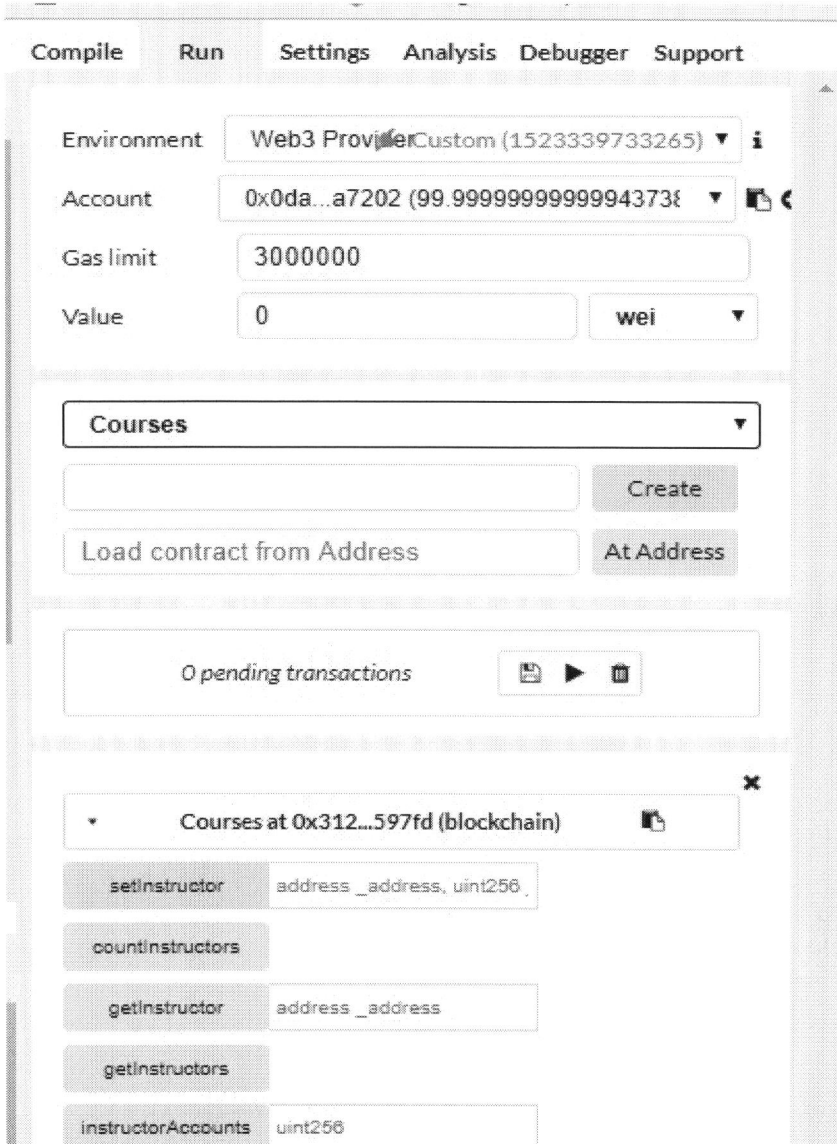

At this point, our smart contract is ready to go. So, what next?

It is now time to simulate the DApp to give us a live experience on the Ethereum Blockchain. The next section delves deeper to provide you with a solid

123

understanding of deploying smart contracts.

#3: Deploying smart contracts

For us to deploy our smart contract, we require the following tools:

- **MetaMask**: MetaMask is a Google Chrome plugin that facilitates the interaction between the browser and the Ropsten Test Network;
- **Ropsten Test Network**: It is a platform that accurately simulates the experience of DApp on the live Ethereum Blockchain.

To use the Ropsten Test Network, you have to install a lite-server to allow the MetaMask to inject an instance of the Web3.Js API.

Here is how to install the lite-server:

- Launch the Bash Terminal and navigate to the project's folder that you've been using.
- Type the following command at the command prompt and hit the Enter key:

```
npm install lite-server --save-dev
```

- Next, launch your code editor and inside the `package.json` file, add this code under scripts:

```
"scripts": {
  "dev": "lite-server"
},
```

- Run the following command to launch the lite-server:

```
npm run dev
```

124

The above command automatically loads the index.html file that you've been working on, in your browser at the localhost address.

Next, we install MetaMask by proceeding as follows:

- Launch the Google Chrome
- On the extreme top left taskbar, click on Apps>Webstore.
- Type MetaMask in the search button and hit the Enter key:
- Click on "Add to Chrome" to Install the MetaMask as Google Chrome extension. Here is what you should see:

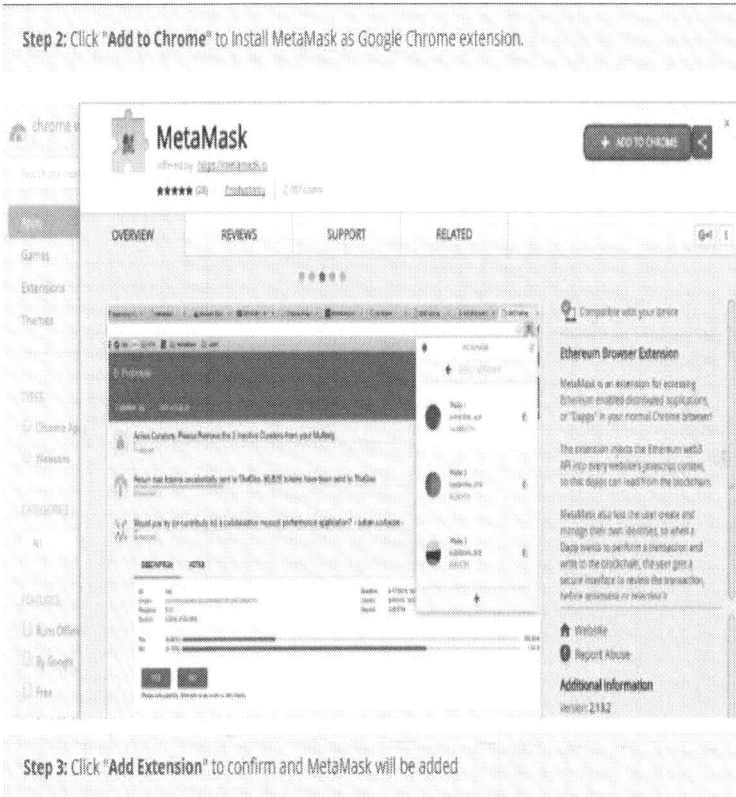

Step 2: Click "**Add to Chrome**" to Install MetaMask as Google Chrome extension.

Step 3: Click "**Add Extension**" to confirm and MetaMask will be added

- Click on "Add Extension" to confirm installing MetaMask.

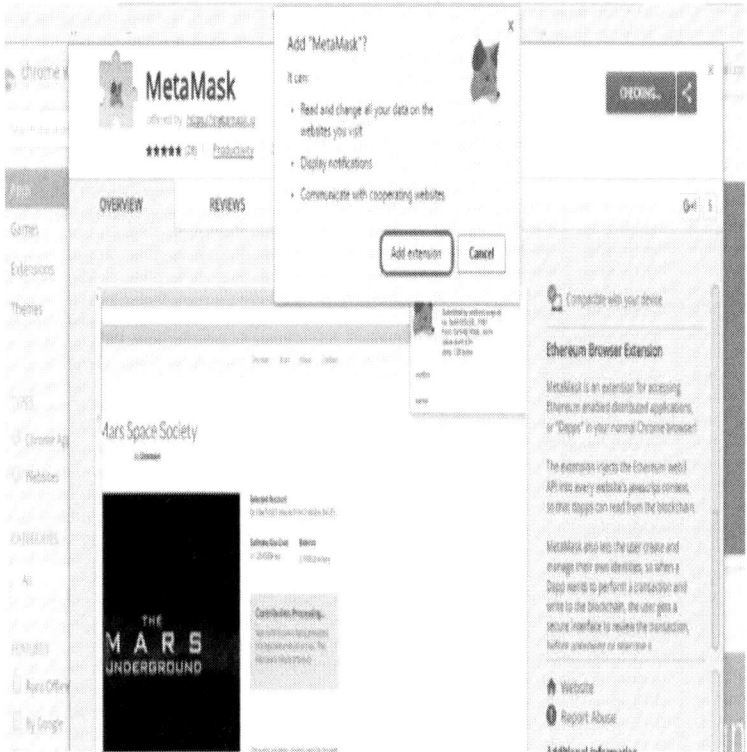

u can see that MetaMask is added by the little fox logo that shows up on the top right corner

Once you install the MetaMask, you can now create your own wallet by proceeding as follows:

- Click on the MetaMask logo at the extreme top right of the Google Chrome's taskbar.

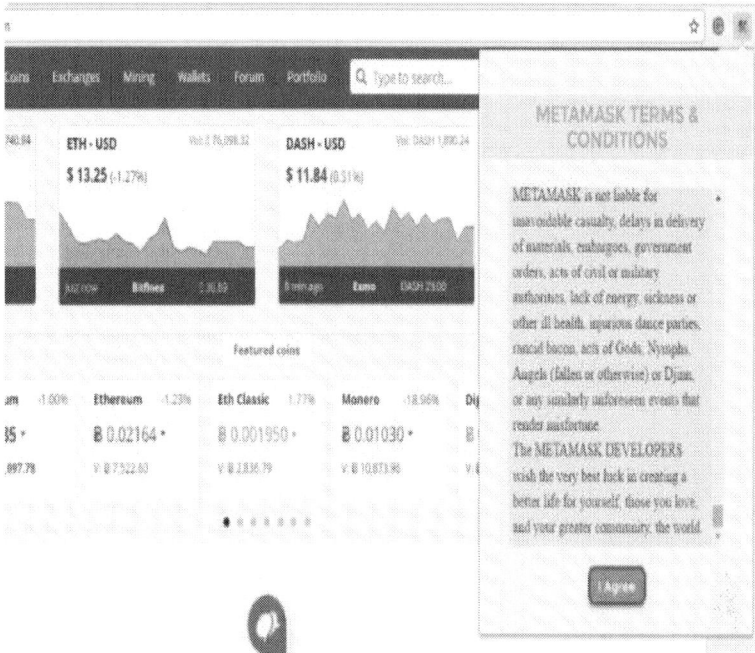

- Read and agree to the Terms and Conditions
- Click on 'New Vault."

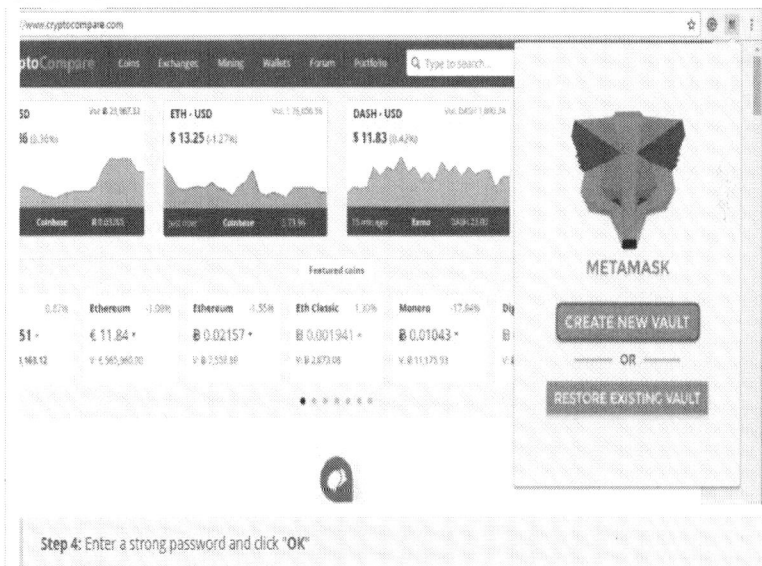

Step 4: Enter a strong password and click "OK"

- Generate a passphrase

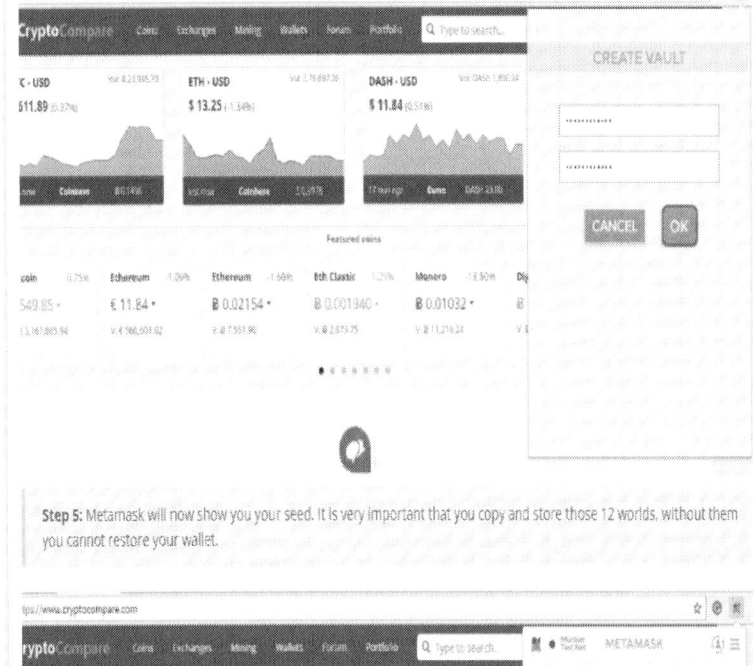

Step 5: Metamask will now show you your seed. It is very important that you copy and store those 12 worlds, without them you cannot restore your wallet.

- Click OK.

Deploying the smart contract on the Ropsten Test Network

The current status of the Web3 UI project will only work if you are using a different version of the contract. However, since we have updated the smart contract, we must go back to Remix IDE and redeploy it. Proceed as follows:

- Launch the Remix Editor and Click on the "Run" link
- Under the Environment tab, alter to "Injected Web3." This will use the Metalmark's injected Web3 instance, which will deploy the smart contract on the Ropsten Test Network.

128

- Now click on "Create" to deploy the contract. Navigate to the Compile tab and copy the ABI code from the Details button.
- Open the project in your code editor and paste the new API code into the following line:

```
var            CoursetroContract        =
web3.eth.contract(PASTE ABI HERE);
```

Next, we modify the actual HTML code to accommodate the changes we have made on first and last name fields:

```
<div class="container">
    <h1>Coursetro Instructor</h1>
    <span id="countIns"></span>
    <h2 id="instructor"></h2>
    <span id="insTrans"></span>
    <hr>
    <img                          id="loader"
src="https://loading.io/spinners/double-
ring/lg.double-ring-spinner.gif">
    <label   for="firstName"   class="col-lg-2
control-label">First Name</label>
    <input id="firstName" type="text">
    <label    for="lastName"    class="col-lg-2
control-label">Last Name</label>
    <input id="lastName" type="text">
    <label for="age" class="col-lg-2 control-
label">Instructor Age</label>
    <input id="age" type="text">
    <button               id="button">Update
Instructor</button>
</div>
```

The next line in the JavaScript underneath the contract address is where you define the variable for the event. Here is a slight change that you can make:

```
// Change this:
var instructorEvent = Coursetro.Instructor();
// To this:
var               instructorEvent           =
Coursetro.instructorInfo({},'latest');
```

This is simply telling the event that you only want the latest event when the instructor has been added. You should also change the ".watch()" function associated with that event as follows:

```
instructorEvent.watch(function (err, result) {
    if (!err) {
        if          (result.blockHash        !=
$("#instrans").html())
            $("#loader").hide();
        $("#insTrans").html('Block      hash:      '
+result.blockHash);

$("#instructor").html(web3.toAscii(result.args.fN
ame) + ' ' + web3.toAscii(result.args.lName) + '
(' + result.args.age + ' years old)');
    } else {
        $("#loader").hide();
    }
});
```

Next, we'll use a new function called ".toAscii" because the names are now bytes types and not strings. Underneath this code, you can add a new section that will give you a count of your instructors as follows:

```
Coursetro.countInstructors((err, res) => {
    if (res)
        $("#countIns").html(res.c      +        '
Instructors');
});
```

130

Next, we'll update the click event to work with the new method in the contract:

```
$("#button").click(function() {
    $("#loader").show();

Coursetro.setInstructor(web3.eth.defaultAccount,
$("#age").val(),
$("#fName").val(),$("#lName").val(),  (err,  res)
=> {
        if (err)
            $("#loader").hide();
});
```

Lab challenge

Deploy the following smart contract on a Ropsten Test Network:

```
pragma solidity ^0.4.19;
contract Revenue {
    address public creator;
    mapping(uint => address) public holders;
    uint public numholders;
        event   Disburse(uint   _amount,   uint
_numholders);
        function Revenue(address[] addresses) {
        creator = msg.sender;
        numholders = addresses.length;
        for (uint i=0; i< addresses.length; i++)
{
            holders[i] = addresses[i];
        }
    }
        function  shareRevenue()  payable  returns
(bool  success)   {
        uint amount = msg.value / numholders;
        for (uint i=0; i<numholders; i++) {
```

```
            if      (!shareholders[i].send(amount))
revert();
        }
        Disburse(msg.value, numholders);
        return true;
    }

        function kill() {
        if      (msg.sender      ==      creator)
selfdestruct(creator);
    }
}
```

Summary

This chapter has examined how inheritance—a concept of OOP languages—and deployment are handled in Solidity. In a sense, inheritance allows new objects to be created based on the characteristics of existing objects. In Solidity, you must always start inheriting by defining the owner address and modifier which offers capabilities to access specific functions.

We have learned that the EVM does not compile the Solidity code as it is. It has to be compiled down to the EVM byte-code that provides extra information about the smart contract. The 2 properties that are essential for deploying smart contracts are ABI(Application Binary Interface) which is a standard protocol of interacting with smart contracts on the Ethereum Blockchain and the Byte-code which the EVM eventually executes.

Deploying smart contracts on EVM requires the MetaMask and the Ropsten Test Network. Whereas

MetaMask is a Google Chrome plugin that facilitates the interaction between the browser and the Ropsten Test Network; the Ropsten Test Network is a platform that accurately simulates the experience of DApp on the live Ethereum Blockchain.

References

1. https://coursetro.com/posts/code/103/Solidity-Inheritance-and-Deploying-an-Ethereum-Smart-Contract
2. https://medium.com/@JusDev1988/part-2-deploying-smart-contracts-in-the-browser-with-web3js-and-vanilla-javascript-f85214113fec
3. https://medium.com/@guccimanepunk/how-to-deploy-a-truffle-contract-to-ropsten-e2fb817870c1
4. https://blog.bankex.org/how-to-buy-ethereum-using-metamask-ccea0703daec

Chapter 7: Embark Framework and Its Deployment

Prerequisite

This chapter will include programming assignments in Web3.Js. No prior experience with Embark framework is required. However, a solid understanding and mastery of the following concepts are required:

- Blockchain and smart contracts (Covered in chapter 1);
- JavaScript programming;
- HTML5 and CSS;
- Solidity programming (Covered in chapter 1 and2);
- Linux commands; and
- Basic Linux administration skills

Theory

In the previous chapters, we've been exploring how to program smartcontracts on EVM with Solidity. We have used Web3.Js to interact with both local and remote Ethereum nodes using the conventional HTTP and IPC connections. Through various libraries bundled in Web3.Js, you have learned how to code, compile, run and even deploy smart contracts.

But what if you wanted to go deeper?

If your goal is to write bigger DApps, use multiple files, test, debug and use a versioning system, then you may consider the Embark framework. Embark is a framework for developing and deploying DApps. Since DApps are server-less HTML5 programs, they combine several decentralized technologies.

Embark integrates with several technologies to make this possible. Among these technologies are:
- EVM Blockchains;
- IPFS (Interplanetary File System); and
- Decentralized communication platforms (Whisper and Orbit);
- Web technologies

#1: EVM Blockchain

With Embark framework, you can:
- Automatically deploy the smart contracts and make them accessible in the JavaScript code. Here, Embark will automatically track the changes and redeploy the smartcontracts (if required) and the Dapp;
- Make the smartcontracts to be available in JavaScript with Promises;
- Perform Test Driven Development with the smartcontracts using JavaScript;
- Track the deployed smartcontracts and deploy them when needed;
- Manage different Blockchains such as testnets, private net, and livenet; and

135

- Manage complex platform of interdependent smartcontracts.

#2: IPFS

IPFS (Interplanetary File System) is a network and protocol conceived to create a peer-to-peer (P2P) and content-addressable scheme for storage and sharing of hypermedia in distributed systems. In other words, IPFS is a decentralized storage protocol. At its core, the IPFS is simply versioned file system that takes files, store and manages them by keeping track of their versions over time.

It also accounts for how the stored and shared files move across the distributed system. With Embark framework, you can:
- Easily store and retrieve data on the DApp via EmbarkJS; and
- Deploy the full program to Swarm or IPFS.

#3: Decentralized Communication (Whisper, Orbit)

These are communications protocols and toolsets that allows DApps built on the Ethereum protocol stack to communicate to each other. They include all the aspects of the distributed hash table and point-to-point communications platform which would enable programs on the Ethereum platform to talk with one another.

They can also be used to efficiently store and retrieve data for use in the Ethereum programs and contracts. With Embark framework, you can easily send and receive messages via channels in the P2P in Whisper or Orbit

#4: Web Technologies

Embark framework can help you achieve the following goals:

- Integrate the DApp with any web technology such as Foundation or React; and
- Use any build tool or pipeline such as grunt, gulp, and Web pack to create and manage your DApp.

As you can see, Embark is a useful framework that you can't ignore if you want to code and deploy larger DApps that require integration of multiple technologies. In the next section, we describe how you can get started with Embark.

Embark libraries and languages available

Embark can build and deploy contracts coded in both Solidity and Vyper. It will also make the smart contracts to be available on the client side via its EmbarkJS and Web3.Js frameworks. However, to use Vyper, you must first install Vyper on your PC. This implies that doing Vyper contract.v.py will be possible in Embark.

Using smart contracts in Embark framework

#1: Using Contracts

Embark automatically takes care of the deployment

process for you by setting up all the required JavaScript bindings. Consider the smart contract below:

```
# app/contracts/simple_storage.sol
pragma solidity ^0.4.19;
contract Simple_storage {
  uint public stored_data;
  function    Simple_storage(uint    initialValue)
public {
    stored_data = initialValue;
  }
  function set(uint m) public {
    stored_data = m;
  }
  function get() view returns (uint retVal) {
    return stored_data;
  }
}
```

The Embark framework will automatically convert the above code and make it available in JavaScript as follows:

```
# app/js/index.js
Simple_storage.methods.set(100).send({from:
web3.eth.defaultAccount});
Simple_storage.methods.get().call().then(function
(value) { console.log(value.toNumber()) });
Simple_storage.methods.stored_data().then(functio
n(value) { console.log(value.toNumber()) });
```

For each smart contract and environment, you can specify the gas costs and arguments as follows:

```
# config/contracts.json
{
  "development": {
    "gas": "auto",
    "contracts": {
```

```
      "Simple_storage": {
        "args": [
          1000
        ],
        "gas": 8000000
      }
    }
  }
}
```

If you are using many smart contracts, you can pass a reference to another contract as $ContractName and Embark will automatically replace this with the appropriate address for the smart contract. You can also define the interfaces and choose not to deploy the smart contract as follows:

```
# config/contracts.json
{
  ...
  "development": {
    "contracts": {
      "SimpleStorage": {
        "args": [
          1000,
          "$My_storage"
        ]
      },
      "My_storage": {
        "args": [
          "initial string"
        ]
      },
      "MyMainsmartcontract": {
        "args": [
          "$Simple_storage"
        ]
      },
      "MyContractInterface": {
```

```
                "deploy": false
            }
        }
    }
    ...
}
```

You can now deploy multiple instances of the same smart contract as follows:

```
# config/contracts.json
{
  "development": {
    "contracts": {
      "Currency": {
        "deploy": false,
        "args": [
          1000
          ]
      },
      "Usd": {
        "instanceOf": "Currency",
        "args": [
          2000
          ]
      },
      "MyCoins": {
        "instanceOf": "Currency",
        "args": [
          2000
          ]
      }
    }
  }
}
  ...
}
```

#2: EmbarkJS

The EmbarkJS is a JavaScript library that is meant to abstract and facilitate the implementation of DApps. Here is how you can specify and import Embark into your DApp project:

```
var mySmartContract = new EmbarkJS.Contract({abi:
abiObject, address: "0x123"});
mySmartContract.methods.get().call().then(functio
n(value)     {     console.log("value     is     "     +
value.toNumber) });
```

To use events in your smart contract, use the code below:

```
mySmartContract.events.eventName({from:web3.eth.a
ccounts},      'latest').then(function(event)      {
console.log(event)
```

The client side deployment is automatically available in the Embark for existing contracts as follows:

```
Simple_storage.deploy([args],
{options}).then(function(anotherSimple_storage)
{});
```

The above code can manually be defined as follows:

```
var mySmartContract = new EmbarkJS.Contract({abi:
abiObject, code: code});
mySmartContract.deploy([args],
{options}).then(function(anotherMyContractObject)
{});
```

Therefore, you can define your gas limit as follows:

```
mySmartContract.deploy([1000,                "seconde
argument"],                                    {gas:
```

```
8000000}).then(function(anotherMySmartContractObj
ect) {});
```

#3: Embark communication

For Whisper, use the following code syntax:

```
EmbarkJS.Messages.setProvider('whisper')
```

For Orbit, you will need to use the IPFS from master and execute it as:

```
ipfs daemon --enable-pubsub-experiment
```

Here's how you can set the provider:

```
EmbarkJS.Messages.setProvider('orbit',    {server:
'localhost', port: 5001})
```

To listen to messages, use the code below:

```
EmbarkJS.Messages.listenTo({topic:    ["subject1",
"subject2"]}).then(function(message)                {
console.log("received: " + message); })
```

To send messages, you can use the plain text as follows:

```
EmbarkJS.Messages.sendMessage({topic:   "Subject",
data: 'Hello Ernesto!'})
```

#4: Testing

Embark has a testing library which you can rapidly run and test your smart contracts in the EVM under the test/. Embark uses Mocha by default, however you can use any framework that you are familiar with.

Here is a simple JavaScript definition of tests:

```
# test/simple_storage_spec.js
describe("Simple_storage", function() {
before(function(done) {
this.timeout(1);
var smartContractsConfig = {"Simple_storage": {
args: [1000]}
 };
EmbarkSpec.deployAll(smartContractsConfig, done);
  });
  it("should      set      constructor      value",
function(done) {
    Simple_storage.stored_data(function(err,
result) {
      assert.equal(result.toNumber(), 100);
      done();
    });
  });
it("set storage value", function(done) {
Simple_storage.set(15, function() {
Simple_storage.get(function(err, result) {
assert.equal(result.toNumber(), 150);
done();
      });
    });
  });
});
```

Aim

So far, we have used Web3.Js to interact with both local and remote Ethereum nodes using the conventional HTTP and IPC connections. Through various libraries bundled in Web3.Js, you have learned how to code,

compile, run and even deploy smart contracts. The aim of this chapter to demonstrate how Embark framework can help you create and manage DApps across multiple technologies.
Let's get started.

Lab Task

The aim of this lab task is to install and get started with Embark. Here is the workflow:

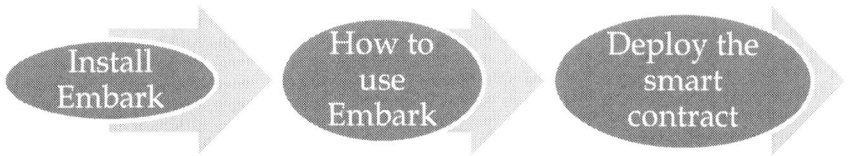

#1: Installing Embark

Here are minimum requirements that will get you started with Embark:
- geth (version 1.6.7 or higher);
- NodeJS (version 6.9.1 or higher); and
- Npm

You may also need to install the following apps even though they are optional:
- Ganache-cli (successor to TestRPC)
- IPFS

Chapter 2 of this book has delved in deeper to explain how to install geth, NodeJS, and npm. Here are steps to follow in case you want to install Embark:

- Open the Terminal and type the following command at the command prompt:

```
npm -g install embark
```

- Hit the Enter key and wait for the installation to complete.
  Here is what you should see:

If you haven't installed ganache-cli, type the following command and hit the Enter key:

```
npm -g install ganache-cli
```

Now, that you have installed Embark, what next?
Well, it's time to begin creating DApps in it.

#2: How to use Embark

You can create a sample working DApp by typing the following commands at the prompt:

```
embark demo
cd embark_demo
```

Here is what you should get:

```
 Keisha@Oddillia: ~

Keisha@Oddillia:~$ embark demo
Initializing Embark Template....
Init complete

App ready at embark_demo
-------------------
Next steps:
-> cd embark_demo
-> embark blockchain or embark simulator
open another console in the same directory and run
-> embark run
For more info go to http://github.com/iurimatias/embark-framework
Keisha@Oddillia:~$ _
```

To run a real Ethereum node for development purposes, type the following command and press the Enter key:

```
embark blockchain
```

Here is what you should see:

```
Keisha@OddiNix: ~/embark_demo                                    –  □  X
INFO [04-08|11:37:10] Maximum peer count              ETH=0 LES=0 total=0
INFO [04-08|11:37:10] Starting peer-to-peer node      instance=Geth/v1.8.2-stable-b8b9f7f4/linux-amd64/go1.9.4
INFO [04-08|11:37:10] Allocated cache and file handles database=/home/Keisha/embark_demo/.embark/development/datadir/geth/chaindata cache=76
8 handles=1024
WARN [04-08|11:37:11] Upgrading database to use lookup entries
INFO [04-08|11:37:11] Initialised chain configuration config="{ChainID: <nil> Homestead: 1 DAO: <nil> DAOSupport: false EIP150: <nil> EIP15
5: <nil> EIP158: <nil> Byzantium: <nil> Constantinople: <nil> Engine: unknown}"
INFO [04-08|11:37:11] Database deduplication successful deduped=0
INFO [04-08|11:37:11] Disk storage enabled for ethash caches dir=/home/Keisha/embark_demo/.embark/development/datadir/geth/ethash count=3
INFO [04-08|11:37:11] Disk storage enabled for ethash DAGs dir=/home/Keisha/.ethash                       count=2
INFO [04-08|11:37:11] Initialising Ethereum protocol  versions="[63 62]" network=12301
INFO [04-08|11:37:11] Loaded most recent local header number=0 hash=b6cfea…d22ab3 td=0
INFO [04-08|11:37:11] Loaded most recent local full block number=0 hash=b6cfea…d22ab3 td=0
INFO [04-08|11:37:11] Loaded most recent local fast block number=0 hash=b6cfea…d22ab3 td=0
INFO [04-08|11:37:12] Regenerated local transaction journal transactions=0 accounts=0
INFO [04-08|11:37:12] Starting P2P networking
INFO [04-08|11:37:12] RLPx listener up                self="enode://df71ccc1e31c2243f5cc1ade31a8a91757b98fb81c45beb2151205549e3b7620aaebbd681
6efcd3b5eedd2655cefdbf3e0206102686d6064e0badc2a629ed29c1c7@[::]:30303?discport=0"
INFO [04-08|11:37:12] started whisper v.5.0
INFO [04-08|11:37:13] IPC endpoint opened             url=/home/Keisha/embark_demo/.embark/development/datadir/geth.ipc
INFO [04-08|11:37:13] HTTP endpoint opened            url=http://localhost:8545                          cors=http://localho
st:8000 vhosts=localhost
INFO [04-08|11:37:13] WebSocket endpoint opened       url=ws://127.0.0.1:8546
INFO [04-08|11:37:14] Unlocked account                address=0x74De2a2b65F382927628a4432faFA11c0F25fdE9
INFO [04-08|11:37:14] Transaction pool price threshold updated price=18000000000
INFO [04-08|11:37:14] Etherbase automatically configured address=0x74De2a2b65F382927628a4432faFA11c0F25fdE9
INFO [04-08|11:37:15] Starting mining operation
INFO [04-08|11:37:15] Commit new mining work          number=1 txs=0 uncles=0 elapsed=19.006ms
== Funding account
INFO [04-08|11:37:15] Updated mining threads          threads=0
INFO [04-08|11:37:15] Transaction pool price threshold updated price=18000000000
INFO [04-08|11:37:15] Starting mining operation
```

To use an ethereum RPC simulator type the following command and hit the Enter key:

```
embark simulator
```

By default, the Embark Blockchain mines a minimum amount of Ether which will only be done when new transactions come in. This is necessary to keep a low CPU. You can configure this option at "config/blockchain.json." To run a real Ethereum node requires at least 2GB of free memory.

To automatically deploy your contracts, update their

147

JavaScript bindings and deploy DApps to a local server, type the following command in another window and hit the Enter key:

```
embark run
```

Here is what you should see as the Embark dashboard:

The dashboard indicates the state of the smart contract, the environment that you are using, and what Embark is doing at the time.

a. *How to create a new DApp*

Type the following commands and press the Enter key to create a new DApp:

```
embark new ApplicationName
cd ApplicationName
```

For example, to create a new DApp named Cryptokitty, just type:

```
embark new Cryptokitty
cd Cryptokitty
```

Here is what you should now see:

```
Keisha@Oddillia:~$ embark demo
Initializing Embark Template....
Init complete

App ready at embark_demo
-------------------
Next steps:
-> cd embark_demo
-> embark blockchain or embark simulator
open another console in the same directory and run
-> embark run
For more info go to http://github.com/iurimatias/embark-framework
Keisha@Oddillia:~$ embark new Cryptokitty
Initializing Embark Template....
Init complete

App ready at Cryptokitty
Keisha@Oddillia:~$ cd Cryptokitty
Keisha@Oddillia:~/Cryptokitty$
```

b. *DApp Structure*

All DApps that you'll be creating will have the following structure:

```
Application
|___ contracts/
|___ html/
|___ css/
|___ js

Config
|___ blockchain.json
|___ contracts.json
|___ storage.json
|___communication.json
|___ webserver.json

Test
|___ #contracts tests
```

DApp

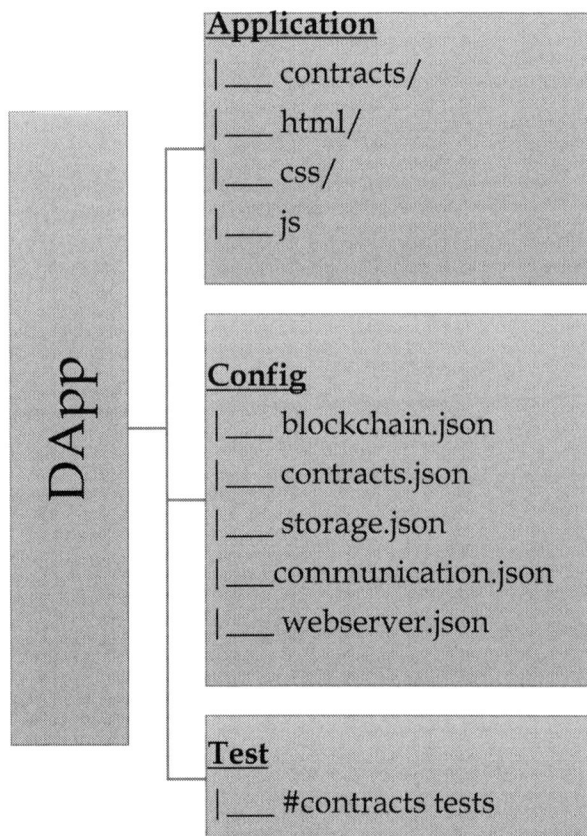

The Solidity files in the smart contracts directory will automatically be deployed when you type `Embark run` command. In addition, any changes to files will automatically be updated in DApp while changes to the smart contracts will result in redeployment and subsequent updates of their JavaScript bindings.

When you open the app/contracts folder of the demo, here is what you will see:

As you can see, the CSS, images and js directories contain sources for building the web applications which will interact with the Ethereum Blockchain. To check what the Embark demo web DApp does, simply launch your browser and point it to http://localhost:8000/

If you have some DApps already using port 8000, you can modify the port number used by Embark in the directory "config/webserver.json." Here is what you should see:

151

Embark - Usage Example

Blockchain   Decentralized Storage (IPFS) ●   P2P communication (Whisper/Orbit) ●

1. Set the value in the blockchain

| 10 | Set Value |

Once you set the value, the transaction will need to be mined and then the value will be updated on the blockchain.

2. Get the current value

current value is

Get Value

Click the button to get the current value. The initial value is 100.

3. Contract Calls

Javascript calls being made:

As you can see, we now have a simple UI to interact with the smart contract. For instance, you can now set the value stored in the smart contract, get it and see the function calls that have been made to interact with it. Next, we explore how you can deploy smart contracts under Embark framework.

#3: How to deploy smart contracts

As mentioned in the previous chapter, a DApp creates an interface that you can use to interact with the smart contract and the EVM. Therefore, any DApp will always have 2 essential components:

- UI: The user interface allows normal users to interact with the smart contract and is developed from HTML5, CSS, and JavaScript.
- Smart contract: The smart contract is coded using Solidity and resides on the Ethereum Blockchain and manages the logic of the application.

152

In this exercise, we will create a DApp—to be called blogging—whose functionalities include:

- Registering a user
- Posting messages from users
- Listing all the accounts
- Listing all the messages from users

Therefore, we will write 2 smart contracts; the first one will be the actual program that stores all the accounts and let the user register while the second one will be the user accounts. Proceed as follows:

Launch your Terminal and type the following command:

```
embark new blogging
cd blogging
```

The above commands generate the directories for our DApp. You can now load the directory in your favorite IDE create the first smart contract. We will name this contract as `blogging.sol` and store it in the directory app/contracts. Navigate to the directory app/contracts and use your favorite editor (I like nano) to create blogging.sol as follows:

```
nano blogging.sol
```

Here is what you see:

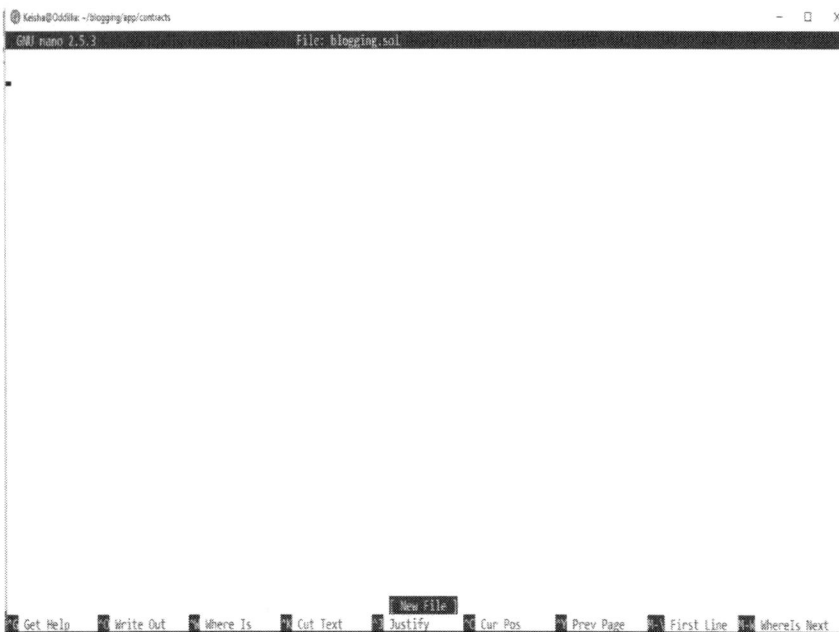

Just copy/paste the code below into the window as follows:

```solidity
pragma solidity ^0.4.19;
contract bloggingAccount {
   struct Post{
     uint timestamps;
     string messages;
   }
    uint public number_Posts;
   address public owner;
   mapping (uint => Post) posts;
   modifier isOwner() {
     require(owner == msg.sender);
     _;
   }
   function bloggingAccount(address _owner) {
     owner = _owner;
     number_Posts = 0;
   }
```

```
function post(string messages) isOwner() {
  require(bytes(messages).length <= 160);
  posts[number_Posts].timestamps = now;
  posts[number_Posts].messages = messages;
  number_Posts++;
}
 function get_Post(uint postId) constant returns
(string messages, uint timestamps) {
  require(postId < number_Posts);
  messages = posts[postId].messages;
  timestamps = posts[postId].timestamps;
}
function  getOwnerAddress()  constant  returns
(address _owner) {
  return owner;
}
function  get_NumberPosts()  constant  returns
(uint _number_Posts) {
  return number_Posts;
}
}
```

Now, deploy this contract by typing the command below:

```
ganache-cli
embark simulator
```

The above command initiates the Blockchain. In another window, type the following command:

```
embark run
```

Your contract will be deployed as follows:
To check if the smart contract works, access it from the console by typing the following:

155

```
bloggingAcount.get_NumberPosts().toNumber()
bloggingAccount.getOwnerAddress
```

You can also try the following function calls:
```
bloggingAccount.getNumberPosts().toNumber()
bloggingAccount.post("Embark is nice to use")
bloggingAccount.getPost(0)[0]
bloggigAccount.getPost(0)[1].toNumber()
```

Lab Challenge

Implement and deploy the following smart contract using Embark framework:

```
pragma solidity ^0.4.19;
contract BoardVotes {
    string titles;
    string descs;
    function castVote(string _title, string desc)
public {
        titles = _title;
        descs = description;
    }
    function getPublics() public constant returns
(string, uint) {
        return;
    }
    }
```

Summary

In this chapter, we have learned that writing bigger DApps, using multiple files, testing, debugging and a versioning system, requires a mastery of the Embark framework. Embark is a framework for developing and deploying DApps. Embark integrates with several technologies such as EVM Blockchains, IPFS, Decentralized communication platforms (Whisper and Orbit), and web technologies to provide a framework for developing and deploying DApps.

References

1. https://www.npmjs.com/package/embark#structuring-application
2. https://ethereumdev.io/deploying-contract-embark-framework/
3. https://ethereumdev.io/deploying-contract-embark-framework/

Chapter 8: Solidity and Smart Contracts' Testing

Prerequisites

This chapter will comprise of programming assignments in Web3.Js. Emphasis is placed on testing DApps under the Embark framework. No prior experience with testing is expected. However, a solid understanding and mastery of the following concepts are a must:

- Blockchain and smart contracts (Covered in chapter 1);
- JavaScript programming;
- HTML5 and CSS;
- Solidity programming (Covered in chapter 1 and2);
- Embark framework and installation procedures (Covered in chapter 6);
- Linux commands; and
- Basic Linux administration skills

Theory

This chapter explores the process of testing your smart contracts after coding. Therefore, even before we dive in, a brief overview of software testing is crucial moving forward.

Overview of software testing

Like it or not, errors will always occur in your smart

contract no matter how keen you are on programming. Despite your best efforts to write comprehensive smartcontracts in Solidity, it's virtually impossible to avoid the bugs.

Software testing the process of examining parts of your smart contracts to make them bug-free. It entails testing various modules in the smartcontracts and identifying bugs that may cause instability when the smartcontract is deployed. In most cases, software testing an incremental process in which you enhance the existing smart contract—not starting from scratch— by making changes to the contract in bits.

In most languages, you'll begin the process of testing the software by finding out any solution that is working. At the initial stages of the programming, determining the best solution is almost next to impossible. This is because you'll be having various solutions in mind on how the problem can be tackled.

This can lead to high chances of the smart contracts turning out with many bugs than anticipated. The process of writing the smartcontract by identifying solutions that work and enhancing them is formally called Test Driven Development (TDD). And TDD has become the most extensive approach to software development that you can use in any language, not just Solidity.

In TDD, you'll start by developing an example case of the smart contract that can be used to ensure the contract works or not. Once the test case has been created, you will then focus on writing the smartcontract that passes the test of functionality with few or no bugs. If the test case passes, you'll then proceed on refactoring it or improving its code so that it executes faster, is more readable and is adhering to best practices in programming.

The process of the smart contract will assume 2 primary stages:
- Creating a test plan; and
- Creating a test case.

a. Test plan

A test plan is a strategy that you'll employ during smart contracts testing. It's simply a guideline that will be used in the entire process of smart contracts testing. A test plan may contain the following information:
- Development environment of the smart contract;
- The hardware specification;
- OS specifications;
- The scope of the smart contract;
- The limitation of the testing; and
- The testing approach.

Next, you'll proceed to the actual testing—which involves generating a test case.

b. Test case

A test case simply documents all the aspects of the smart contract after conducting the different levels of testing. A test case can have the following information:
- A set of the test data;
- The pre-conditions in the smart contract;
- The expected results of the smartcontract; and

- The postconditions of the smartcontract.

The report that is generated from the test case must factor in the bugs and any defects that have been identified between the expected outcome and actual output in the modules of the smart contracts. Next up, we explore how you can test smart contracts in Solidity.

Writing the tests
Consider the example below:

```
pragma solidity ^0.4.19;
contract MySmartContract {
    uint public somenumber;
    /*the function below stores numbers greater
than 10. */

    function MySmartFunction()
    {
        somenumber = 34;
    }
    function storeNum(uint mynum)
        public returns (bool success)
    {
require(mynum > 10);
somenumber = mynum;
    return true;
    }
}
```

Here, we begin by storing number 24. Using the function storeNum (), we only want to store numbers that are greater than 10. Now, to get our bearings correct, let's go over and see how the Solidity test will be assembled together.

First, you'll need to import the files below:

```
import "Embark/tests.sol"
import "Embark/DeployedAddresses.sol"
import "../contracts/MySmartContract.sol"
```

It is important to note that the Solidity tests must start with "Test"—uppercase "T", to identify it in Embark framework as a test. Similarly, all the Solidity test functions must also start with "test."

Let's start with a simple Solidity test case:

```
import "Embark/tests.sol";
import "Embark/DeployedAddresses.sol";
import "../contracts/MySmartContract.sol";
contract TestMyContract {
function testInitialStoredValue() {
MySmartContract          mycontracts          =
MySmartContract(DeployedAddresses.MyContract());
uint expected = 24;
Assert.equal(mycontract.somenumber(),   expected,
"First number set must be 24.");
     }
}
```

When you run the Embark test, you'll see the test passed. As it's expected, our initial value of somenumber is 24 as laid out in the `MySmartContract.sol` and Ganache was busy.
Now that we have the simple Solidity test concluded, let's see how we can test our ultimate goal—the 3 functions (assert (), require (), and revert ()). Here is the code for testing our ultimate goal:

```
import "Embark/Assert.sol";
import "Embark/DeployedAddresses.sol";
import "../contracts/MySmartContract.sol";
contract TestMySmartContract {
```

```
function testTheThrows() {
    MySmartContract      mycontract      =      new
MySmartContract();
    ThrowProxy           throwproxys      =      new
ThrowProxy(address(mycontract));

MySmartContract(address(throwproxys)).storeNum(7)
;
    bool r = throwproxys.execute.gas(20000)();
Assert.isFalse(r, "Must be false because is should
always throw!");
}
function testNoThrows() {
    MySmartContract      mycontract      =      new
MySmartContract();
    ThrowProxy           throwproxys      =      new
ThrowProxy(address(mycontract));

MySmartContract(address(throwproxys)).storeNum(22
);
    bool r = throwproxys.execute.gas(200000)();
    Assert.isTrue(r,  "Must  be  true  because  is
should always throw!");
}
}

// Proxy contract for the testing throws
contract ThrowProxy {
  address public target;
  bytes data;
function ThrowProxy(address _target) {
target = _target;
  }

  //prime the data via the fallback function.
  function() {
    data = msg.data;
  }
  function execute() returns (bool) {
    return target.call(data);
  }
```

```
}
```

You can now see from the above code that we now have a `ThrowProxy` smart contract included in the `TestMySmartContract.sol`. You can also note that the `ThrowProxy` is now storing the address of its target (which is the contract that we want to test for the throws.

This coincides with the first 2 lines of the `testTheThrow` () function since you must first create a new `MySmartContract` and then enter that address into the `ThrowProxy`. Now, there is a basis for testing assert (), require () and revert () in an Embark test environment. The next test `testNoThrow` () will work in exactly the same manner as the previous `testTheThrow` ()— preparing our call data throw and using call () to check whether or not the function completed running.

A decent practice in the product business is composing tests for code. The tests need to cover the highlights of your code and declare that everything is filling in as anticipated. As we are composing keen gets that can manage cash, composing tests is an extremely vital assignment for us. The Embark Framework offers a truly rich condition for testing our shrewd contracts.

The majority of smart contracts that you'll be creating will be managing either tokens or cryptocurrencies. Therefore, it is imperative that you test the code to ensure it conforms to the client specifications. In this chapter, we will use the following tools to use our smart contracts:

- ***Embark framework***: Embark is a framework for developing and deploying DApps; and
- ***Mocha***: Mocha is a feature-rich JavaScript test framework that runs on Node.Js and in the browsers simplifying asynchronous process testing. The Mocha tests run in a serial fashion, allowing for accurate and flexible reporting while mapping any uncaught exceptions to the correct test cases.

Installing Mocha is simple. Just launch your Terminal and type the following command, press the Enter key and wait for the installation process to complete:

```
npm install -g mocha
```

Aim

The majority of smart contracts that you'll be creating will be managing either tokens or cryptocurrencies. Therefore, it is imperative that you test the code to ensure it conforms to the client specifications. In this chapter, we will use the following tools to use our smart contracts:

- ***Embark framework***: Embark is a framework for developing and deploying DApps; and
- ***Mocha***: Mocha is a feature-rich JavaScript test framework that runs on NodeJS and in the browsers simplifying asynchronous process testing. The Mocha tests run in a serial fashion, allowing for accurate and flexible reporting while mapping

any uncaught exceptions to the correct test cases.

Here is the workflow that we'll use:

#1: Install Mocha

Installing Mocha is simple. Just launch your Terminal and type the following command, press the Enter key and wait for the installation process to complete:

```
npm install -g mocha
```

#2: Create the smart contract

Since we already have a smart contract, we don't have to start from scratch. In case you are stumbling on this section for the first time, here is the smart contract:

```
pragma solidity ^0.4.19;
contract bloggingAccount {
   struct Post{
     uint timestamps;
     string messages;
   }
    uint public number_Posts;
   address public owner;
   mapping (uint => Post) posts;
   modifier isOwner() {
```

```
    require(owner == msg.sender);
    _;
  }
  function bloggingAccount(address _owner) {
    owner = _owner;
    number_Posts = 0;
  }

  function post(string messages) isOwner() {
    require(bytes(messages).length <= 160);
    posts[number_Posts].timestamps = now;
    posts[number_Posts].messages = messages;
    number_Posts++;
  }
   function get_Post(uint postId) constant returns
(string messages, uint timestamps) {
    require(postId < number_Posts);
    messages = posts[postId].messages;
    timestamps = posts[postId].timestamps;
  }
  function  getOwnerAddress()  constant  returns
(address _owner) {
    return owner;
  }
  function  get_NumberPosts()  constant  returns
(uint _number_Posts) {
    return number_Posts;
  }
 }
```

The above smart contract is already saved in the Embark directory app/contracts as `blogging.sol`. You can navigate to the directory app/contracts and use your favorite editor such as nano to check its contents as follows:

```
nano blogging.sol
```

#3: Testing the smart contract

We will test the following functionalities of the smart contract:
- Whether it is empty when initialized;
- Whether it creates a contract when a user registers; and
- Whether it retrieves a contract made by a user.

To start us off, create a new file in the test directory test/blogging_spec.js. Navigate to the test directory and type the following command:

```
nano blogging_spec.js
```

The above command will launch the nano Editor. Copy/paste the following code inside the nano Window:

```
var assert = require('assert');
var Embark = require('embark');
var EmbarkSpec = Embark.initTests();
var web3 = EmbarkSpec.web3;
```

The above code simply imports the tools and libraries that we need to test our smart contract. Using Mocha, we will now describe the tests and deploy all of the contracts in the project as follows:

```
describe("blogging", function() {
 before(function(done) {
   this.timeout(0);
   EmbarkSpec.deployAll({}, done);
 });
 //The tests go here
})
```

Here is the first test:

```
it("Should     be     empty     after     deployment",
function(done) {
   blogging.getNbAccounts(function(err, result) {
     assert.equal(result.toNumber(), 0);
     done();
   });
 });
```

The above code tests to confirm whether blogging is indeed empty.

Next, we will check if an account is really generated by calling the register function:

```
it("A    user    can    register    for    an    account",
function(done) {
   blogging.register({gas:900000},    function(err,
result) {
     blogging.getNbAccounts(function(err,  result)
{
       assert.equal(result.toNumber(), 1);
       done();
     });
   });
 });
```

Finally, we test if the smart contract has a correct address and function to access the contracts:

```
it("Retrieving account address should be similar
and different from 0x0", function(done) {
   web3.eth.getAccounts(function(err, accounts) {
     blogging.getAccount(accounts[0],
function(err, accountaddress) {
       blogging.getAccountId(0,      function(err,
accountaddressid) {
         assert.equal(accountaddress,
accountaddressid);
```

```
        assert.notEqual(accountaddress,
'0x0000000000000000000000000000000000000000');
        done();
      });
    });
  });
});
```

Here is the complete code:

```
var assert = require('assert');
var Embark = require('embark');
var EmbarkSpec = Embark.initTests();
var web3 = EmbarkSpec.web3;
describe("blogging", function() {
 before(function(done) {
   this.timeout(0);
   EmbarkSpec.deployAll({}, done);
 });
 it("Should    be    empty    after    deployment",
function(done) {
   blogging.getNbAccounts(function(err, result) {
     assert.equal(result.toNumber(), 0);
     done();
   });
 });
it("A    user    can    register    for    an    account",
function(done) {
   blogging.register({gas:900000},    function(err,
result) {
     blogging.getNbAccounts(function(err, result)
{
       assert.equal(result.toNumber(), 1);
       done();
     });
   });
 });
it("Retrieving account address should be similar
and different from 0x0", function(done) {
   web3.eth.getAccounts(function(err, accounts) {
```

```
      blogging.getAccount(accounts[0],
function(err, accountaddress) {
        blogging.getAccountId(0,      function(err,
accountaddressid) {
        assert.equal(accountaddress,
accountaddressid);
        assert.notEqual(accountaddress,
'0x0000000000000000000000000000000000000000');
        done();
      });
    });
  });
 });
})
```

Now that we have defined the test file, we can proceed to test the smart contract. To execute the tests in Embark Framework, type the following command and press the Enter key:

```
embark test
```

Lab challenge

Use the Truffle framework to deploy and test the smart contract that we have been using in this chapter.

Summary

This chapter has explored the process of testing smart contracts in Solidity. Software testing the process of examining parts of your smart contracts to make them bug-free. It entails testing various modules in the smart contracts and identifying bugs that may cause instability when the smart contract is deployed. In Solidity, you can use Embark and Mocha to test your smart contracts.

References

1. https://ethereumdev.io/testing-solidity-smart-contracts/
2. https://mochajs.org/
3. http://truffleframework.com/docs/getting_started/testing
4. https://github.com/mochajs/mocha

Chapter 9: Contracts Management with Factories

Prerequisites

This chapter will place emphasis on smart contract management with factories. A solid understanding and mastery of the following concepts are required:

- Blockchain and smart contracts (Covered in chapter 1);
- JavaScript programming;
- HTML5 and CSS;
- Solidity programming (Covered in chapter 1 and2);
- Linux commands; and
- Basic Linux administration skills

Theory

Over time you have developed a set of smart contracts that you frequently use to make the transactions more efficient. But, as you begin to collect a bunch of smart contract files, the time it takes to manage them can increase significantly. In a sense, your once simple development platform can become messy; especially if you are not having some levels of consistency and common patterns in the development process.

Contract management can help you deploy efficient smart contracts with a proven sustainability and maintainability framework. Here are the pain points that may require efficient contract management:

- You are the sole maintainer of the smart contract (or a small group of developers uses the code that requires constant changes;
- There are a no wider department or company-wide procedures in place to cover your smart contract;
- The smart contract base tends to include so many stand-alone scripts without various multi-file Solidity apps.
- The majority of smart contract files have between 30 and 300 lines of Solidity code.
- The smart contract is a one-off system or is being used as part of a periodic reporting and analysis.

Because Solidity is so expressive, you can perform a complex task in only a few numbers of lines of code. As you begin to develop your own smart contract repository, you'll realize that you have ended up with dozens of Solidity scripts that work great. But if you don't use them frequently, maintenance will start to consume more and more of your development time.

There are 3 techniques of smart contract management:

- Dynamic contract factories;
- Counterfactual contract deployment; and
- Arbitrary code execution on deployed contracts.

#1: Dynamic contract factories

The conventional processes of managing smart contracts can be problematic. For instance, the moment creates a new contract using `new Contract(...)` anywhere in Solidity code, the contract's byte-code is automatically added at the end of the main contract byte-code. This has 2 primary problems:

- It increases the amount of gas that will be required to execute the contract on the Blockchain: You will pay more to deploy the factory and all its children in the same transaction; and
- The byte-code will not be modifiable in any way by the smart contract: This can limit the development if you're working on the smart contract as a group.

Dynamic contract factories can help you deploy contracts in Solidity without using the `new Contract (...)` method. Here, you simply create opcodes directly and gives it a dynamic byte array as follows:

```
contract DynamicFactory {
  function    deployedCode(bytes    _code)    returns
(address deployedAddress) {
    assembly {
      deployedAddress   :=   create(0,   add(_code,
0x20), mload(_code))
      jumpi(invalidJumpLabel,
iszero(extcodesize(deployedAddress)))
// It should jump if there is no code at the
addresses
    }
    ContractDeployed(deployedAddress);
  }
    event                   ContractDeployed(address
deployedAddress);
}
```

To deploy a smart contract this way, you would call the `deployedCode` function with the byte-code of the contract and deploy it as an argument specifying the input data of the contract transactions.

175

#2: Counterfactual contract deployment

The fact that you can deterministically know what addresses the not-yet-deployed contracts will have can allow you to pre-fund contracts before their existence. You can even hard-code their addresses even if the contracts have not been developed. In Ethereum, smart contracts are always deployed in an address which is a function of that account's and its nonce—a random number which can only be used once—as follows:

```
contractAddress    =    sha3(rlp_encode([address,
nonce]))
```

The last 20 bytes of the SHA3 protocol of the list is composed of the address and the nonce that has been encoded in the smart contract. For private-key based accounts, the nonces have to be increased each time transaction are sent from that account. In the case of the smart contract, it is only increased when it creates an operation (each time the smart contract generates another contract).

The Solidity function that determines all the addresses that the contract will deploy functions based on the code below:

```
contract Counterfacts is DynamicFactory {
  function addressForNonces(uint8 nonce) constant
returns (address) {
    if (nonce > 127) throw;
    return          address(sha3(0xd6,          0x94,
address(this), nonce));
  }
  function Counterfacts() payable {
    firstDeployments = addressForNonce(uint8(1));
```

```
    bool b = firstDeployments.send(msg.value);
  }
  address public firstDeployments;
```

If the above smart contract is deployed, it will send whatever value it was deployed with to the account address that the first contract was deployed with. Therefore, the moment you execute `deployedCode`, it will be automatically converted into a smart contract.

#3: Arbitrary code execution on the deployed contracts

To apply the arbitrary code execution on the deployed smart contracts, you must first define a Fixable base class which specifies which contracts want to be fixed as follows:

```
contract Fixable is DynamicFactory {
  function executeCodes(bytes _code) {
    execute(deployedCode(_code));
  }
  function executes(address fixer) {
    if (!canExecuteArbitraryCode()) throw;
    assembly {
      calldatacopy(0x0, 0x0, calldatasize)
      let  a  :=  delegatecall(sub(gas,  100000),
fixer, 0x0, calldatasize, 0, 0)
      return(0, 0)
    }
  }
  function    canExecuteArbitraryCodes()    returns
(bool);
}
```

Smart contracts can be made to specify the circumstances that they will execute code as follows:

```
contract BrokenContracts is Fixable {
```

```
  function BrokenContracts() {
    broken = true;
    creator = msg.sender;
  }
  function   canExecuteArbitraryCodes()   returns
(bool) {
    return broken && msg.sender == creator;
  }
  bool public broken;
  address public creator;
}
```

Now the Fixer contract (which inherits from `BrokenContracts`) will have the same storage, and it can easily change it as follows:

```
contract Fixer is BrokenContracts {
  function executes(address fixer) {
    broken = false;
  }
}
```

Next up, we explore how to manage multiple smart contracts with factories

Aim

The aim of this section is to find out how multiple contracts can be managed with factories.

Lab Task

Here is the workflow for our lab task:

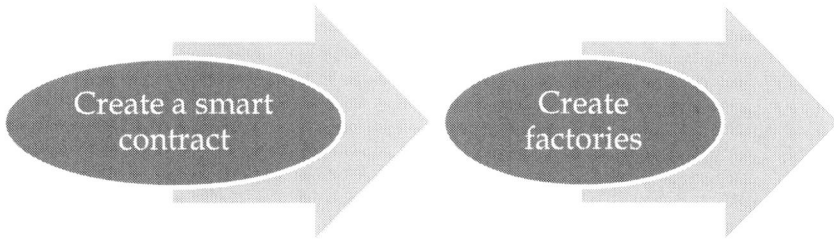

#1: Create a smart contract

Consider the following smart contract:

```solidity
pragma solidity ^0.4.19;
contract Counters {
    /* define variable counter of the type uint */
    uint counter = 0;
    /* this executes when the contract is run */
    function increments() public {
        counter = count + 1;
    }
    /* used to read the value of counter */
    function getCounts() constant returns (uint)
{
        return counter;
    }
}
```

#2: Create factories

We will now use the previous counters contract to create a platform where users create their own counters. Here, we will create a CountersFactory which will now manage all the other Counters. Obviously, CountersFactory must contain a mapping that associates an owner to the address of his/her counter contract.

179

Here is a code that generates the mapping:

```
mapping(address => address) counters;
```

Whenever any user wants to use the counter system to have his own counter he/she will request the creation of that counter as follows:

```
function createCounters() public {
    if (counters[msg.sender] == 0) {
        counters[msg.sender]          =          new
Counters(msg.sender);
    }
}
```

Notice that we are passing to the constructor the address of the owner to transfer the ownership of the caller. In the constructor of the generated smart contract, the `msg.sender` will now refer to the address of the contract factory. In the increment function, we first check if the user has already registered the contract. If he/she has already registered, we call the increment function from the smart contract as follows:

```
function increments() public {
    require (counters[msg.sender] != 0);

Counter(counters[msg.sender]).increment(msg.sende
r);
}
```

Because mapping usually stores the address of the smart contract, you'll need to cast the address to the Counters contract type. Storing the address of the smart contract and not its direct reference will allow you to check if the contract was initialized or not using the null address.

Finally, to read the value of the counters, you'll take the address of the user as an argument of the counter as follows:

```
function    getCounts(address    account)    public
constant returns (uint) {
    if (counters[account] != 0) {
        return
(Counters(counters[account]).getCounts());
    }
}
function    getCounts(address    account)    public
constant returns (uint) {
    if (counters[account] != 0) {
        return
(Counters(counters[account]).getCounts());
    }
}
```

Here is the complete smart contract:

```
pragma solidity ^0.4.19;
contract Counters {
    address owner;
    address factory;
    uint count = 0;
    function Counters(address _owner) {
        owner = _owner;
        factory = msg.sender
    }
    modifier isOwner(address _caller) {
        require(msg.sender == factory);
        require(_caller == owner);
        _;
    }
    function  increments(address  caller)  public
isOwner(caller) {
```

181

```
        counter = counter + 1;
    }
    function getCounts() constant returns (uint)
{
        return counter;
    }
}
contract CounterFactory {
    mapping(address => address) counters;
    function createCounters() public {
        if (counters[msg.sender] == 0) {
            counters[msg.sender]        =        new
Counter(msg.sender);
        }
    }
    function increment() public {
        require (counters[msg.sender] != 0);

Counter(counters[msg.sender]).increment(msg.sende
r);
    }
    function  getCounts(address  account)  public
constant returns (uint) {
        if (counters[account] != 0) {
            return
(Counters(counters[account]).getCounts());
        }
    }
}
```

Lab challenge

Explain how you'll manage the following smart contract using factories:

```solidity
pragma solidity ^0.4.8;

contract RevenueSharing {
    address public creator;
    mapping(uint => address) public shareholders;
    uint public numShareholders;

    event Disburse(uint _amount, uint _numShareholders);

    function RevenueSharing(address[] addresses) {
        creator = msg.sender;
        numShareholders = addresses.length;
        for (uint i=0; i< addresses.length; i++) {
            shareholders[i] = addresses[i];
        }
    }

    function shareRevenue() payable returns (bool success)  {
        uint amount = msg.value / numShareholders;
        for (uint i=0; i<numShareholders; i++) {
            if (!shareholders[i].send(amount)) revert();
        }
        Disburse(msg.value, numShareholders);
        return true;
    }

    function kill() {
        if (msg.sender == creator) selfdestruct(creator);
    }
}
```

Summary

Contract management can help you deploy efficient smart contracts with a proven sustainability and maintainability framework. Because Solidity is so expressive, you can perform a complex task in only a few numbers of lines of code. Therefore, it can be problematic to manage complex smart contracts using Solidity.

Fortunately, you can manage your smart contracts using Dynamic contract factories, Counterfactual contract deployment or arbitrary code execution on deployed contracts.

References

1. https://ethereumdev.io/manage-several-contracts-with-factories/
2. https://blog.aragon.one/advanced-solidity-code-deployment-techniques-dc032665f434
3. http://pbpython.com/best-practices.html

Chapter 10: IPFS Online Files Hosting

Prerequisites

IPFS has been touted as the next-generation peer-to-peer file system and web technology. This chapter delves deeper to provide a big-picture view of how you can leverage IPFS to host your smart contracts. No prior experience of IPFS is required. However, you must have basic knowledge of Linux commands and basic Linux administration skills.

Theory

IPFS (Interplanetary File System) is a network and protocol conceived to create a peer-to-peer (P2P) and content-addressable scheme for storage and sharing of hypermedia in distributed systems. In other words, IPFS is a decentralized storage protocol. At its core, the IPFS is simply versioned file system that takes files, store and manages them by keeping track of their versions over time.

In some ways, this is akin to the original aims of the Internet; however, IPFS is actually more like a single BitTorrent swarm exchanging the Git objects. IPFS could become the new major subsystem of the Web. If implemented right, it could even complement or replace the current HTTP.

185

At its core, IPFS is a versioned file system which can take files and manage, and store them on the web and then tracks versions over given time. In this regard, IPFS accounts for how the versioned files move across the web since it is a distributed file system. This file system provides properties such as:

- Websites which are completely distributed;
- Websites which have no origin server;
- Websites which can run entirely on the client side browsers; and
- Websites which don't have any servers attached to them

Content addressing

Rather than referring to the objects (pictures, videos, and articles) by which server they are stored on, the IPFS refers to any file by its hash. For instance, if in your browser you want to access a particular web page then IPFS will just ask the entire network "does any node have this file which corresponds to this hash?"

A node on the IPFS that has the hash returns the file allowing you to access it. IPFS uses the content addressing mechanisms at the HTTP layer. Instead of creating an identifier that addresses files by location, IPFS address it by a representation of the content itself. In other words, the content determines the address. The idea is to take the file, hash it cryptographically and generate a small and secure representation of the file that people will access.

The diagram below summarizes the mechanics of IPFS:

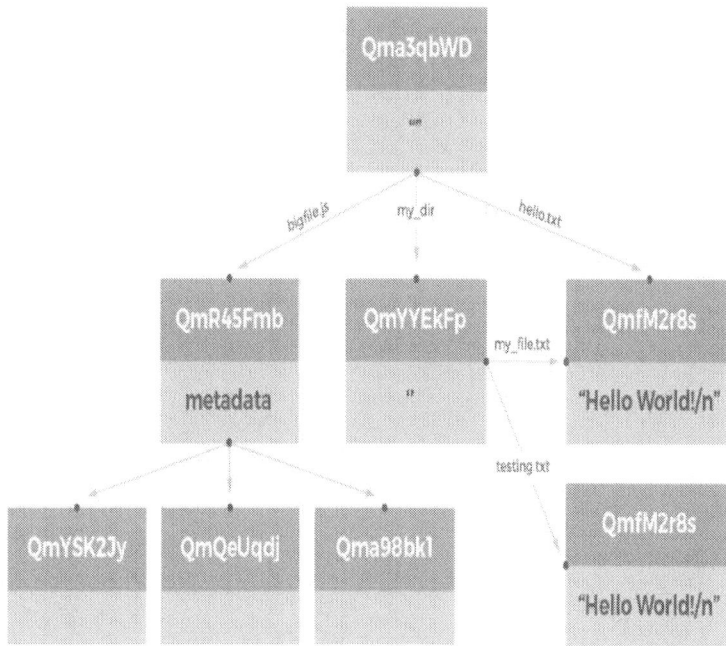

Source: Medium.com

HTTP verses. IPFS

HTTP is a standard protocol for the web where the identifier is simply the location of the server. In a sense, HTTP makes it easy to locate computers hosting the file and communicate with them. This is useful and generally works well but not in the offline state or large distributed databases such as Blockchain projects where you want to reduce the load across the network.

DApps that you need to be completely decentralized will be hosted online using the IPFS. The issue is that once you add a file to the system, it disappears after around 24 hours if no one else has it stuck. It gets junk gathered by the system.

Your site will be online on the hash returned however it will go down following 24 hours on the off chance that you don't keep it online with your own IPFS hub.

IPFS separates the steps into 2 parts:

- Identifying the file with the content addressing; and
- Going out and finding it

When you have the hash, you'll simply connect to the corresponding nodes and download that file. The result is P2P (peer-to-peer) overlay which gives you faster routing. It also accounts for how the stored and shared files move across the distributed system.

IPFS Objects

IPFS is a P2P system that retrieves and shares the IPFS objects. An IPFS object is a data structure with 2 basic fields:

- Data: Data is a blob of unstructured binary data that are less than 256 kB; and
- Links: Links are an array of the Link structures that connects to other IPFS objects.

A Link structure has 3 main data fields:

- Name: This specifies the name of the link;
- Hash: This is the hash of the linked IPFS object; and
- Size: The cumulative size of the linked IPFS object and primarily used for optimizing the P2P network.

At present, IPFS is implemented in Go, with a JavaScript implementation which exists and the Python implementation that is still in progress as of writing this. IPFS can be regarded as:

- A protocol;
- A file system;
- A web;
- A modular system;
- A cryptosystem; and
- A peer-to-peer network

#1: Protocol
- IPFS is a protocol because:
- It specifies how the content-addressed file system should work;
- It coordinates the content delivery;
- It combines Kademlia, BitTorrent, and Git

#2: Filesystem
IPFS is a file system because:
- It has files and directories; and
- It has a mountable file system through its FUSE platform.

#3: Web
IPFS is a web because:
- It can access files and documents from the Internet;
- Files are accessible through http protocol at https://ipfs.io; and
- Its hash-addressed content guarantees authenticity

#4: IPFS is modular
IPFS is a modular system because:
- It is routing layer;
- It creates a connection layer across any network; and

- It uses bit-torrent-inspired block exchange

#5: IPFS is a cryptosystem
IPFS is a cryptosystem because:
- It uses cryptographic-hashes to generate content addressing; and
- It applies block-level de-duplication

#6: IPFS is P2P network
IPFS can be regarded as a P2P network because:
- It enables worldwide P2P transfer of files; and
- It has an entirely decentralized architecture with no central point of failure

Next, we describe what is required to get us started with IPFS.

Aim

The aim of this section is to help you understand how to use IPFS to host your online files.

Lab Task

In this lab task, we will install IPFS and describe how to use it. Here is the workflow:

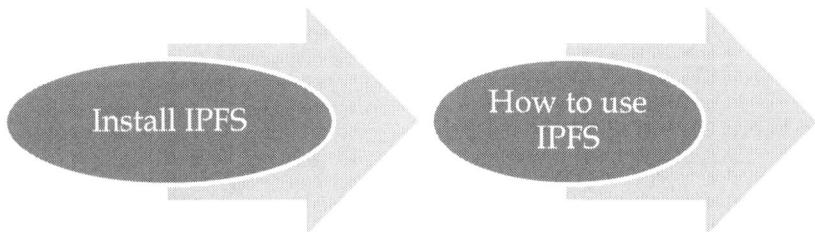

#1: Install IPFS

Here are quick steps to install IPFS on Ubuntu:
- Launch your Terminal
- Update the system by typing the following command

```
sudo apt-get update
apt-get install build-essential
```

- Install Go by typing the following command

```
sudo apt-get install golang-go
nano /etc/profile.d/go.sh
```

- Now download IPFS by downloading it into a directory of your choice by typing the command below:

```
wget                    https://dist.ipfs.io/go-
ipfs/v0.4.10/go-ipfs_v0.4.10_linux-
386.tar.gz
```

- Unzip the downloaded file as follows:

```
tar xvfz go-ipfs_v0.4.10_linux-386.tar.gz
```

- Install the IPFS as follows:

```
sudo mv go-ipfs/ipfs /usr/local/bin/ipfs
```

#2: How to use IPFS

Launch IPFS node by typing the following command:
```
ipfs init
```

Next, launch a daemon procedure (an IPFS hub that will communicate with the system) and manage the transfer documents on the web by typing the command below:

```
ipfs daemon
```

The above command will create a background node. You can exit next message anytime by pressing Ctrl + C since the node is now running in the background. If you want to terminate the background process just type `fg` to bring the process to the foreground. To get the files for hosting want on the IPFS, use `git` as follows:

```
git clone <git-repo>
```

You can now add the files to the platform as follows:

```
ipfs add -r <my-files>
```

Finally, to maintain the files online and prevent them from being garbage-collected, use the pin command as follows:

```
ipfs pin add -r <your-files>
```

The above command will ensure the files remain stored as long as your daemon is executing. To access these files later on, simply point your browser to https://gateway.ipfs.io/ipfs/

Summary

At its core, the IPFS is simply versioned file system that takes files, store and manages them by keeping track of their versions over time. You can use IPFS to store your smart contract files on the web permanently.

References

1. https://gist.github.com/MiguelBel/695d2bd8e135137cfa24c70de1955d80
2. https://dist.ipfs.io/#go-ipfs
3. https://medium.com/@merunasgrincalaitis/how-to-host-your-ipfs-files-online-forever-f0c56b9b5398
4. https://mlgblockchain.com/intro-ipfs.html
5. http://techexpert.tips/ubuntu/installing-ipfs-ubuntu-linux/

Chapter 11: End-To-End Development of DApps

Prerequisites

This chapter will focus on the end-to-end development of DApps. As such, a solid understanding and mastery of the following concepts are required:

- Software development life cycle;
- Blockchain and smart contracts (Covered in chapter 1);
- JavaScript programming;
- HTML5 and CSS;
- Solidity programming (Covered in chapter 1 and2);
- Linux commands; and
- Basic Linux administration skills

Theory

DApps differ from the classical apps in the sense that don't depend on the conventional client-server model. Whereas the client-server model requires a centralized authority to maintain the platform and authorize changes, DApps are fully decentralized systems with no central body to maintain.

Essentially, these apps use a system of computers (called nodes)—which are equal participants—to maintain the network. Because computations are performed at every node independently, all of which complete a record of all the transactions, the DApp platform can provide a number of unique features for the benefit of participating nodes.

In summary here are some key features of DApps:
- They are decentralized: There is no centralized body to manage them;
- They are open source: Their source code is available to the public;
- They offer incentives: The crypto tokens are used to reward the nodes or miners;
- They use consensus protocols and algorithms: These algorithms generate tokens that reward platform participants; and
- They rely on Blockchain: Data is stored cryptographically on the platform.

At present, there are 2 main consensus algorithms that DApps use to reward participation:
- Proof-of-Work (PoW); and
- Proof-of-Stake (PoS)

The PoW is the power behind Bitcoin's consensus mechanism. Besides Bitcoin, PoW is also used by other cryptocurrencies such as Litecoin and Ethereum (for now). In PoW, nodes use their GPUs (Graphical Processing Units) or ASICs (Application Specific Integrated Circuits) — high powered specialized mining hardware—to compute hash algorithms which validates the Blockchain. It is one of the most path-breaking processes in Blockchain systems.

On the other hand, the PoS use deposits of coins (ETH)

to generate the same disincentive, instead of the real-world investments such as hardware and electricity. To successfully mine using the PoS protocol, you must first commit a certain number of coins into a smart contract to act as collateral.

The architecture of DApps

Here is a simplified diagram that summarizes the architecture of DApps:

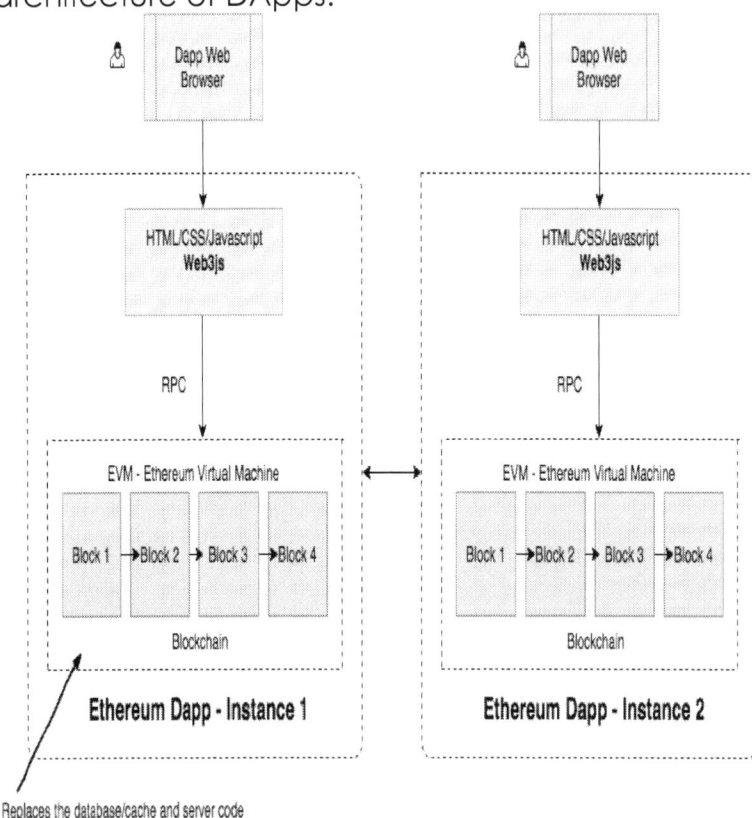

Dapp Web Browser

Dapp Web Browser

HTML/CSS/Javascript
Web3js

HTML/CSS/Javascript
Web3js

RPC

RPC

EVM - Ethereum Virtual Machine

EVM - Ethereum Virtual Machine

Block 1 → Block 2 → Block 3 → Block 4

Block 1 → Block 2 → Block 3 → Block 4

Blockchain

Blockchain

Ethereum Dapp - Instance 1

Ethereum Dapp - Instance 2

Replaces the database/cache and server code

Source: Devteam.space

The straightforward way to understand the differences

between standard apps and DApps is mastering how conventional websites operate. Conventional websites are coded using HTML, CSS, and JavaScript to help render the page to users.

These websites may sometimes grab details using an API (Application Programming Interface) from a back-end database. For instance, when you log in to Twitter, the page calls an API to get your personal data and display them on the web page.

A DApp is similar to a traditional website. Its front end uses the same technology when rendering the web page. However, instead of using an API to connect to the back-end database, a DApp uses a smart contract to connect to the Blockchain in the following sequence:

Here are the main phases of DApps development lifecycle:
- Choosing the technology to be used for DApps development;
- Setting up the project;
- Coding the DApp;
- Deploying and testing the DApp;
- Launching the DApp

The diagram below summarizes the DApp

development lifecycle:

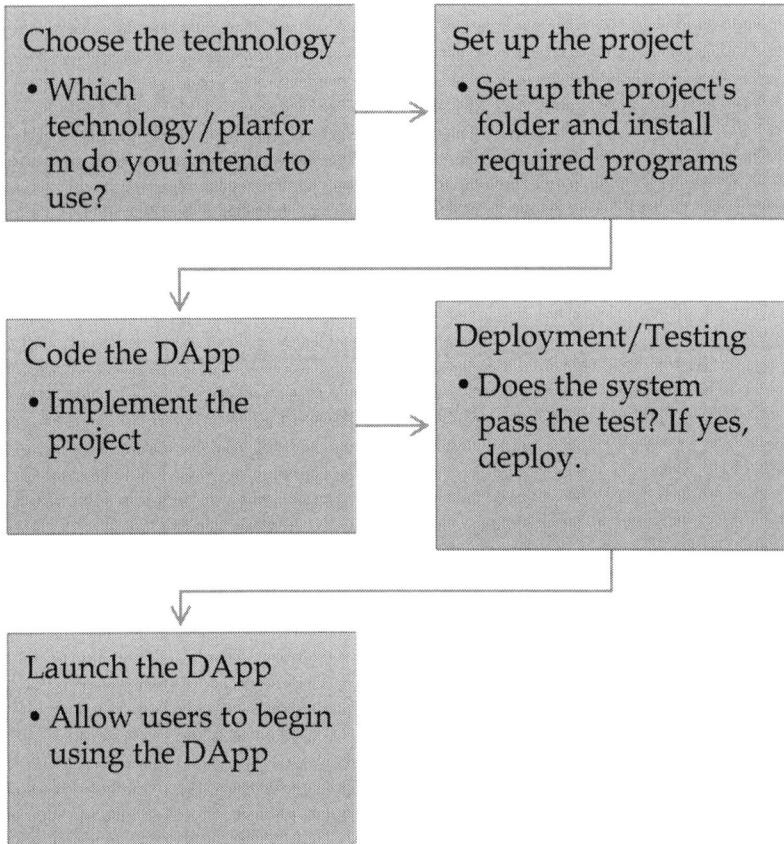

Choose the technology	Set up the project
• Which technology/plarfor m do you intend to use?	• Set up the project's folder and install required programs

Code the DApp	Deployment/Testing
• Implement the project	• Does the system pass the test? If yes, deploy.

Launch the DApp
• Allow users to begin using the DApp

#1: Choose the technology

At this stage, you should consider the technology that you will use. Here is what you have at your disposal:

- Database: So far, we have explored the Ethereum's Testnet Ropsten Blockchain;
- Hosting: So far, we have learned how to use IPFS to obtain free hosting forever on a decentralized platform;

- Frontend: You can use any JavaScript framework that you are familiar with such as Node.Js or React. Js with Webpack. If you are not familiar with any, just use the plain JavaScript;

- Domain name: You can choose Godaddy.com. Or, you could just use some decentralized domain name service such as peername even though it is slow compared to Goddady.com;

- Contract's programming language: So far, we have learned Solidity 0.4.19 which is the most popular among smart contracts languages. But you can also choose Serpent if you are familiar with it;

- Frontend contracts: Here, you should opt for Web3.Js;

- Frameworks: You can select Embark or Truffle to help you compile, run, deploy and test your smart contracts;

- Development server: Here, you should choose Node.Js while developing locally along with ganache-cli.

- MetaMask: You will use MetaMask as the final application as an end user would.

Aim

The aim of this chapter is to present an end-to-end development of DApps. Therefore, we will examine the various steps that can help you create, compile and deploy DApps. Here are the main phases of DApps development lifecycle:

- Choosing the technology to be used for DApps development;
- Setting up the project;
- Coding the DApp;
- Deploying and testing the DApp;
- Launching the DApp

The diagram below summarizes the DApp development lifecycle:

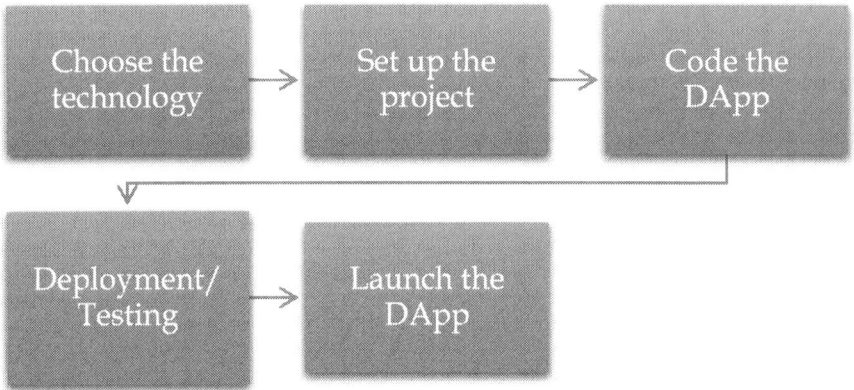

#1: Choose the technology

At this stage, you should consider the technology that you will use. Here is what you have at your disposal:

- **Database**: So far, we have explored the Ethereum's Testnet Ropsten Blockchain;
- **Hosting**: So far, we have learned how to use IPFS to obtain free hosting forever on a decentralized platform;

- **Frontend**: You can use any JavaScript framework that you are familiar with such as NodeJS or React. Js with Webpack. If you are not familiar with any, just use the plain JavaScript;
- **Domain name**: You can choose Godaddy.com. Or, you could just use some decentralized domain name service such as peername even though it is slow compared to Goddady.com;
- **Contract's programing language**: So far, we have learned Solidity 0.4.19, and it is the most popular among smart contracts languages. But you can also choose Serpent if you are familiar with it;
- **Frontend contracts**: Here, you should opt for Web3.Js;
- **Frameworks**: You can select Embark or Truffle to help you compile, run, deploy and test your smart contracts;
- **Development server**: Here, you should choose NodeJS while developing locally along with ganache-cli.
- **MetaMask**: You will use MetaMask as the final application as an end user would.

#2: Lab task (Set up the project)

Here is a quick process to get you started:
- Start off by downloading the current version of NodeJS from their official website https://nodejs.org if you haven't installed it already.

- Next, create a folder on your PC. Inside the folder, open your favorite Terminal or command execute the following command:

```
npm init -y
```

- Now install Embark by executing the command below:

```
npm -g install embark
```

- Alternatively, you can install Truffle framework (if you are familiar with it) by executing the command below:

```
npm i -D -g truffle
```

- Next, execute the following commands:

```
npm i -D webpack react react-dom babel-core
babel-loader    babel-preset-react    babel-
preset-env    css-loader    style-loader    json-
loader web3@0.20.0
```

The above command will install all the tools for creating a front-end of your DApp. As you can see, there are many dependencies because you are implementing a web application by using the latest versions of React. Js and JavaScript.

- Now install the install the Ethereum's Ropsten Testnet by executing the command below:

```
npm i -g http-server
```

The above command installs a light-weight server that you will be using to host your web applications locally on localhost: 8080

- Now, navigate to your project's folder and create a webpack.config.js file. This is the file that will join all the JavaScript files and CSS to generate a single file called `build.js` which has all the JavaScript codes converted into browser-compatible files.

#3: Code the DApp

If you are new to DApp's development, you can start off by learning Solidity, since it is the most straightforward language that you can learn thanks to its similarity to the JavaScript. Solidity is an excellent language for coding smart contracts that your DApps will require.

Before beginning, you have to be familiar with smart contracts, the Blockchain and Solidity syntax. As mentioned earlier in this book, executing and deploying smart contracts directly to the Ethereum Blockchain may cost you money in the form of gas that will go out to miners who processes the transactions.

In the case of Ethereum, gas will be charged as Ether and be deducted from your smart contract account. The next stage is to complete the front-end development. Remember to create a UI that is appealing to end users by keeping in mind its functionality. Just ensure it has all the features that users may want on the platform.

#4: Deploy and test the DApp

The majority of DApps that you'll be creating will be managing either tokens or cryptocurrencies. Therefore, it is imperative that you test the code to ensure it conforms to the client specifications. You can use the following tools to use our smart contracts:

- **Embark framework**: Embark is a framework for developing and deploying DApps;
- **Truffle**: If you are familiar with Truffle, you can use it as a substitute for Embark. Truffle can act your development environment, asset pipeline, and testing framework for Ethereum; and
- **Mocha**: Mocha is a feature-rich JavaScript test framework that runs on NodeJS and in the browsers simplifying asynchronous process testing. The Mocha tests run in a serial fashion, allowing for accurate and flexible reporting while mapping any uncaught exceptions to the correct test cases.

#5: Launch the DApp

Once your DApp has been tested, it will be ready to be launched. To enhance transparency, you can upload it to GitHub. Select a customized domain for the DApp to professionalize, and then the public knows that it is up and running. This will require intensive marketing skills if you are running an ICO.

Even though the hardest part is now behind you, the success of your DApp will depend on regular maintenance and testing to ensure it is fool-proof. As such, you should maintain the same level of diligence and hard work you have used in creating a great DApp in the first place.

Lab challenge

Create a DApp and its associated smart contract of your choice from scratch using any technologies that you are familiar with. Compile, run, deploy, and test the DApp using the technologies that you have mastered in this book.

Summary

This chapter has presented an end-to-end development of DApps. The main stages that you're likely to be involved while developing DApps include choosing the technology, setting up the project, coding, testing and deploying the DApp and launching the DApp.

Congratulations for taking your time to learn smart contracts with Solidity. The fact that you have read the entire book means that you're really interested smart contracts and Solidity programming. Now, this is only the first phase. Remember, you want to be a top-notch Blockchain developer.

Top-notch developers don't give up along the way. Go ahead and practice to conceptualize all the ideas that you have learned in this book. Remember, the rule of thumb in learning any language is practice, and good practice makes perfect.

References

1. https://www.devteam.space/blog/how-to-build-a-decentralized-application-dapps/

2. https://medium.com/@merunasgrincalaitis/the-ultimate-end-to-end-tutorial-to-create-and-deploy-a-fully-descentralized-dapp-in-ethereum-18f0cf6d7e0e
3. https://blockchainhub.net/decentralized-applications-dapps/

10752576R00127

Printed in Great Britain
by Amazon